ADMINISTRATIVE WRITING

MEMOS & LETTERS

Greg Larocque
Heidemarie MacLean
William Marshall

English Program Development Division
Course Development Directorate
Language Training Program
Training Programs Branch
Public Service Commission of Canada

Administrative Writing is part of the English as a second language program of the Public Service Commission of Canada's Language Training Program Branch.

This book was developed and written within the English Program Development Division and produced by the Pedagogical Resources Division.

Editor-in-chief: Howard B. Woods
Editors: Michael Sutton and Jonathan Paterson
Illustrations: John Bianchi
Design and layout: Jonathan Paterson
Word processing: Marianne Ethier and Suzanne Désilets

The authors wish to thank students and teachers in the Public Service Commission's language schools (especially M. Sedgewick, R. Hamilton, A. Mann, D. MacLean, R. Willson, and J. Pederson) for their advice during classroom trials. Special thanks are due to Claire Baldock, Beulah Adler, Shirley Gleason, and Gail Haines for the many hours they spent evaluating exercises, conducting classroom trials, and providing detailed feedback; to Christopher Jones and David Sanders for reading and commenting on draft versions of the manuscript; and to Charlotte Frenette for her valuable contributions to both content and production.

For information on materials developed by the Public Service Commission of Canada for teaching English and French as second languages, please contact:

Pedagogical Production and
Information Division
Course Development Directorate
Asticou Centre
241 Cité des Jeunes
Hull, Québec
Canada K1A 0M7

Available in Canada through

your local bookseller

or by mail from

Canada Communication Group – Publishing
Ottawa, Canada K1A 0S9

Cat. No. SC83-99-5000-1101E
ISBN 0-660-12117-4

PRINTED IN CANADA

INTRODUCTION

Administrative Writing is not a grammar book. Rather, it is a book that teaches wording, organization, and style. Some practice is provided on addresses, formats, abbreviations, etc., but the major focus is on the discourse of administrative correspondence. The questions on the samples can be used as a model for discussion of other samples that students and teachers may bring to class.

Administrative Writing is designed for high intermediate and advanced adult learners. The book, which encourages critical reading and discussion of administrative correspondence, focuses on correct usage and appropriate tone and style. The objectives are:

* to develop word-order skills
* to develop a functional repertoire of appropriate writing gambits
* to develop self-editing and rewriting skills
* to provide wide-ranging memo and letter writing activities

Administrative Writing is divided into four parts. Part One teaches the form and style of memos performing various functions, and Part Two deals with letters. Part Three is a short study of employment applications. Part Four is a study section that comprises 20 sample memos and letters from real administrative situations. Accompanying study questions focus on the analysis of content, style, and tone.

The four parts of *Administrative Writing* may be used sequentially as a complete course; alternatively, Part Four may be used as supplementary material to accompany Parts One and Two. Part Four may also be used separately as a resource for students who want to analyze samples of real administrative writing.

Administrative Writing is intended for classroom use but may also be useful for independent study. The Answer Key contains, as well as answers to the more controlled writing tasks, "possible" and "suggested" answers to many of the more complex tone and style questions. These answers are points of departure for further criticism and discussion.

TABLE OF CONTENTS

Canadian Cataloguing in Publication Data

Larocque, Greg

Administrative writing: memos and letters

Intended for classroom use but may also be useful for independent study.
Biblliography: p.
ISBN 0-660-12117-4
DSS cat. no. SC83-99-5000-1101E

1. Commercial correspondence. 2. Business report writing. 3. Memorandums. I. MacLean, Heidemarie. II. Marshall, William, 1942-   III. Public Service Commission of Canada. Language Training Program Branch.

HF5721.L37 1988   651.7/5   C88-097006-5

PART ONE

MEMOS

The memorandum (memo) is used for communication within a department, often to create a written record.

Tone can vary from informal to very formal, depending on the purpose, the reader, and the writer. In this book we concentrate on neutral and formal tone.

Unit 1

Parts of a Memo

FORMAT

1. Addressee's name and title
2. Sender's name and title
3. Security classification
4. File numbers
5. Date
6. Subject line
7. Body
8. Signature (and title)
9. Reference initials
10. Enclosures
11. Copies

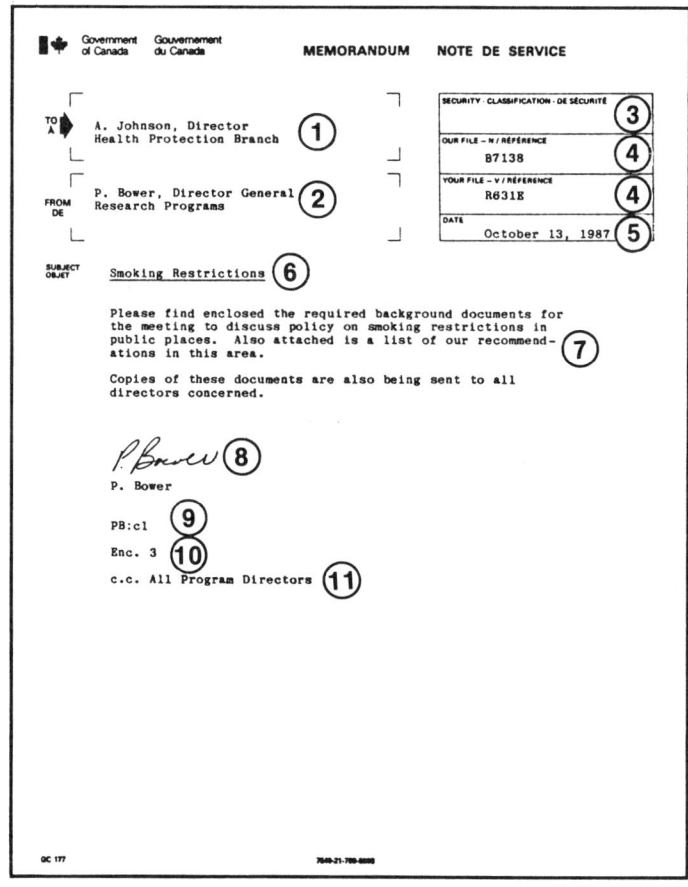

1. Addressee's Name

Since the memo is primarily used for communication within a government department, a full address is not shown. The title of the addressee may or may not be included.

TO   A. Simpson

TO   Andrew Simpson

TO   A. Simpson, Operations Division

TO   A. Simpson, Director
        Operations Division

If a memo is being sent to several individuals, this is specified.

TO   All employees

TO   All staff

TO   All staff, Operations Division

2. Sender's Name

Again, only the name or the name and title of the sender are shown on the FROM line.

3. Security Classification

When necessary, the memo is labelled with one of the government security classifications. These classifications are a) Top Secret, b) Secret, and c) Confidential. However, most memos written by government employees have no security implication, and this line is usually left blank.

4. File Numbers

If applicable, both the originator's and the addressee's file numbers are inserted.

5. Date

The date may be written out in full or abbreviated. For more detailed information and exercises, see page 6.

● ● ● ● ● ● ● ● ● ● ● ● ● ● ● ● ●
TO ECONOMIZE — HANDWRITE   *POUR FIN D'ÉCONOMIE   ÉCRIRE À LA MAIN*

Government   Gouvernement   **ROUND TRIP MEMORANDUM**   **NOTE ALLER RETOUR**
of Canada   du Canada

FROM / DE   Mary Peters ②

File No. (originator) — Dossier n° (source) ④

TO / A   John Burns ①

File No. (addressee) — Dossier n° (destinataire) ④

Subject · Objet   Journal Article ⑥

John, could you phone downtown to the library and reserve the August '86 issue of Video Magazine. I will need the article on pages 22–26 by this Friday, June 11. ⑦

Signature   M Peters ⑧   Date   87-06-07 ⑤   Telephone

Reply · Réponse

Mary, I phoned this morning. Magazine you requested will be sent tomorrow, June 8.

Signature   J Burns ⑧   Date   87-06-07 ⑤   Telephone

1   ADDRESSEE   Please add reply — Keep this copy and return copy 2 to originator.
DESTINATAIRE   Inscrire la réponse — Garder cette copie et expédier la copie 2 à l'initiateur

NOTE

The Round Trip Memorandum includes space for an answer. In comparison with the ordinary memo, it is often much more informal in tone and style. It is not specifically dealt with in this book.

6. Subject Line

A subject heading appears on all memos and tells the reader what the memo is about. For more detailed information and exercises, see pages 7 and 8.

7. Body

Paragraphs tend to be very short and are usually not indented. Paragraphs are not usually numbered, although some departmental manuals suggest it.

8. Signature

All memos are signed or at least initialed by (or for) the sender. If the title of the sender is indicated on the FROM line, it does not have to be repeated below the signature or initials.

9. Reference Initials

The initials of the person who wrote the memo (not necessarily the same as the person who signed the memo) and those of the typist are usually shown in one of the following ways:

GG/ml   GG:ml   Gg/ML

10. Enclosures

If there are any enclosures, this is usually indicated below the reference initials in one of the following ways:

Enclosures   Enc.   Encl.

Att.   Attach.

Sometimes the number of enclosures is also shown:

Enc: (2).

11. Copies

If copies are being sent to persons other than those indicated on the TO line, this should be indicated at the bottom of the page as follows:

c.: All Regional Directors

C.C. See attached list

cc: Joanne Clark

c.c.: John Nevins

DATES

Complete Form

If the date is written out in full, this is usually done in one of the following ways:

August 23, 1985   23 August 1985

The name of the month is always capitalized and a comma is used to separate the day from the year in the first style. Complete forms such as August 1st, 2nd, etc., while sometimes used in running text, are no longer commonly used in the dateline of a memo.

Abbreviated Forms

Both the month and the year may be abbreviated in these ways:

Aug. 23, 85   Aug. 23/85   23 Aug. 85   23 AUG 85

It is also acceptable to use only numbers to represent the date. Traditional Canadian usage is to write the day first, then the month, and then the year:

23/08/85   23-8-85   23/8/85

American practice is to write the month before the day: **8/23/85**

The Canadian Standards Association suggests writing dates with the year in four digits first, then the month in two digits, and finally the day in two digits. The above example would be written as follows: **1985-08-23**

A similar form is also becoming more frequent: **85-08-23**   or   **85/08/23**

If your department recommends a particular style, you should use it.

Writing Abbreviated Forms of Months   **Exercise 1.1**

Write the abbreviated forms for the months of the year.* Remember to capitalize all names of months, even when abbreviated.

January _____	April _____	October _____
February _____	August _____	November _____
March _____	September _____	December _____

Abbreviating Dates   **Exercise 1.2**

Rewrite these dates in the style recommended or most commonly used by your department.

February 14, 1987 _____	January 26, 1985 _____
1988-04-17 _____	21/2/89 _____
25 Aug. 1988 _____	Sept. 5, 1987 _____
8 NOV 1984 _____	4 March 1986 _____
December 2, 1986 _____	14 Feb. 1989 _____

---

* Because May, June, and July have only three or four letters, they are not usually abbreviated. Some departments, however, may have an internal writing system which allows for three-letter abbreviations.

SUBJECT HEADINGS

A subject heading tells the reader what the memo is about and should appear on every memo. It is brief and to the point (as few words as possible) and eliminates the need for a longer introduction in the memo itself.

Capital Letters in Subject Headings

The first letter of all important words is capitalized.

Preparation of Departmental Correspondence

Do not capitalize prepositions (e.g., *to, at, on, from*), articles (*a, an, the*), or conjunctions (e.g., *but, and, or*) unless they are the first word in a subject heading.

The first word in a hyphenated compound is capitalized; capitalize the second word if it is a noun or an adjective or if it is as important as the first word.

By-Hand Mail Service **Long-Term Unit Projects** **Project Co-ordination**

Capitalizing Subject Headings   **Exercise 1.3**

Supply all necessary capital letters for these subject headings.

1. transfer policy _____
2. on-the-job training for PM-01's _____
3. human rights legislation _____
4. delegation of authority _____
5. use of taxis _____
6. end-of-year report _____
7. energy conservation regulations _____
8. unit activities in march 1985 _____
9. copies for canadian and foreign staffs _____
10. 1985-1986 fiscal year close-off _____
11. farewell reception for mr. j. b. jones _____
12. request for lateral transfer _____
13. time-related efficiency index _____
14. cross-analysis of cultural pastimes of franco-ontarians _____

Shortening Subject Headings   **Exercise 1.4**

The following subject headings are all unnecessarily long. Write shorter, more concise headings.

Too Long: *The Eligibility for Long Service Award Certificate of Margaret Forsythe*
Better: *Eligibility for Long Service Award Certificate*

1. A Questionnaire about the Christmas Party for Our Section
   SUBJECT _____
2. A Guide for Research Contractors and Form A for Research Contractors
   SUBJECT _____

3. The Maintenance of the Heating System at Place du Portage Building Complex

SUBJECT _____

4. Some French Language Training Courses to be Given in Regina for the Current Departmental Employees

SUBJECT _____

5. The Issuance of Cheques on an Emergency Basis

SUBJECT _____

Supplying Subject Headings   Exercise 1.5

Read these memos and supply appropriate subject headings. Discuss your headings with another student to see if they can be improved.

1. SUBJECT _____

   The Vocational Guidelines Service was established to provide guidance to employees who are uncertain about the development of their career paths.

   The program offers completely confidential aptitude tests and individual counseling by highly qualified experts.

   If you wish to make use of this free service, please call 979-6985.

2. SUBJECT _____

   It has been brought to my attention that a great many members of the staff fail to lock their filing cabinets at the end of the day.

   This constitutes a serious breach of security (Regulation RS-1002).

   Appropriate measures may be taken against anyone who fails to follow the established security regulations.

3. SUBJECT _____

   There will be a meeting on Wednesday, June 15, at 12:30 in Room 715 to discuss the provisions of the new Collective Agreement. Alice Taylor of Staff Relations will be there to provide information and answer any questions.

4. SUBJECT _____

   Please find attached copies of our monthly reports from July to December 1984. The report for November (pp. 22-26) should be of particular interest to you.

   If you have any questions, please don't hesitate to call me at 984-3213.

Writing Subject Headings   Exercise 1.6

Write subject headings for these situations, supplying names and other details. Exchange headings with another student for comparison and improvement.

1. You wish to inform the employees of your directorate that bicycles may not be brought into individual offices. Instead, they must be left in the racks in the parking lot.

   SUBJECT _____

2. You are to confirm the secondment of a secretary from your section to another section for a period of three weeks.

   SUBJECT _____

3. You are to write a memo to all Section Heads informing them that the weekly meeting will be held on Friday instead of Tuesday.

   SUBJECT _____

4. You wish to request annual leave at a specific time.

   SUBJECT _____

5. You are to inform all employees that the current Director is leaving.

   SUBJECT _____

Predicting the Length of Memos   **Exercise 1.7**

In general, memos present information as precisely and concisely as possible. However, the length of a memo is still an important consideration for the writer. Of course, length will depend on the complexity and importance of the topic. A simple, straightforward topic will require a short memo; a complex topic will require a longer memo.

Read the following subject headings and decide whether you would write a long memo or a short one. Discuss your decisions with the members of your class.

		LONG	SHORT
1.	Research Projects 1980-1986	☐	☐
2.	New Statutory Holiday	☐	☐
3.	Reorganization of Branch	☐	☐
4.	Delegation of Licensing Authority to Provinces	☐	☐
5.	Fire Drill, May 28	☐	☐
6.	Participation in Centraide Campaign	☐	☐
7.	Women in Senior Executive Positions	☐	☐
8.	Charitable Donations to Hospital Expansion	☐	☐
9.	Interpretation of Overtime Regulations	☐	☐
10.	Safety Hazards at Seaway Operating Stations	☐	☐

Unit 2   The Responding Memo

The responding memo is used not only to answer requests or queries, but also to follow up phone calls, meetings, or discussions. It may even be used to respond to policy papers and research reports.

Because the situation and content are given in the original discussion or document, the writer has an idea of any necessary or important vocabulary and of the tone to be set in the response.

There are certain characteristic responding expressions used in writing a responding memo. We will practise these in this unit.

ANSWERING

Much of the writing we do is in response to previous correspondence. There are a number of expressions which point this out to the reader. Here are some of the most common.

Subsequent to ...	**In response to ...**
Further to ...	**In answer to ...**
In reply to ...	

The answering memo does not have to begin with one of the expressions shown above. Instead, it is possible to begin by giving the information and then referring to the previous correspondence.

Example: *We have no objection to the allocation of office space that Carolyn suggested in her memo of June 4.*

Completing Sentences   **Exercise 2.1**

Complete the following sentences by adding your own information. Exchange with another student for correction. Which two of your completed sentences are most formal in tone? Why?

All these opening expressions require mention of the correspondence and additional information in order to form a complete answering sentence.

Example: *In reply to your memorandum of November 10, I regret to inform you that our budget does not allow for the type of training you have proposed.*

1. In response to Carolyn's recent memo regarding allocation of rooms, _____

_____

2. Subsequent to your memorandum on Canadian content in television programming, _____

_____

3. In answer to your memorandum on the introduction of amateur sports programs across Canada,

_____

4. Further to the Deputy Minister's memorandum of January 26, _____

_____

5. In reply to your memo on the advantages of flex-hours, _____

_____

6. In response to your enquiry of 20 January, _____

_____

7. In answer to your question about voluntary overtime, _____

_____

8. In reply to your request for parking space, _____

_____

Responding to a Request   Exercise 2.2

Match the responding expressions on the left with the appropriate segment on the right. Then expand each into a complete sentence. Exchange sentences with another student for correction.

a)   As requested, ...   _____   1.   the Evaluation Branch ...

b)   Following your request, ...   _____   2.   Cabinet Document 83-173-B ...

c)   As requested by ...   _____   3.   George Mitchell, we have completed ...

d)   As requested in ...   _____   4.   I am submitting ...

1. _____

2. _____

3. _____

4. _____

ENDING WITH AN EXPRESSION OF GOODWILL

It is common for memos of this type to end with an expression of goodwill.

I hope this is to your satisfaction.   **I hope this will be useful to you.**
I hope this meets with your approval.   **I hope this will be helpful to you.**

Practising Goodwill Endings   Exercise 2.3

Here are three final paragraphs from real memos. From the context of each statement, select the most appropriate goodwill ending. Discuss your choice with the class. Was your choice a matter of logic, a matter of tone, or both?

1. Perhaps the Canadian Welfare Council and the Ontario Credit Unions, both with headquarters in Toronto, would be able to provide you with the necessary information. I understand that the Welfare Council is most knowledgeable on the subject.

   _____

   _____

2. You will note that the enclosed article contains only the more significant statistics and pinpoints interesting areas of development in New Brunswick in the past year.

   _____

   _____

3. I can only urge you to waive the Standing Offer Contract where only a small amount of money is involved, in order to avoid unnecessary complications and delays.

   _____

   _____

FOLLOWING UP (TELEPHONE CONVERSATIONS)

Information which is exchanged on the telephone sometimes requires written confirmation. Thus, a memo written following a telephone conversation frequently begins with a following-up expression and then a confirming expression.

FOLLOWING UP		CONFIRMING
Following ...,		**this is to confirm ...**
Further to ...,	**+**	**this confirms ...**
With regard to ...,		**I would like to confirm ...**

Example: *Following our telephone conversation of May 1, we would like to confirm that the closing date for competition #88-HW-NMT-I-CCID-721 is extended to June 25, 1988.*

Following Up with Confirmation **Exercise 2.4**

Now write four sentences using the above combinations of expressions and the information below. Exchange your sentences with another student for revision.

1.   The booking of a conference room for a specific time

_____

_____

2.   That an employee is not violating conflict of interest guidelines by consulting on a private project

_____

_____

3.   The completion of a report by a specified date

_____

_____

4.   That summer hours will be in effect for the current year

_____

_____

FOLLOWING UP (GENERAL)

Following-up expressions can be used in connection with documents, instructions, meetings, announcements, and services. The following expressions may be used.

With reference to ...	**In accordance with ...**	**Following ...**
With regard to ...	**In compliance with ...**	**Thank you for ...**
In connection with ...	**Concerning ...**	

Matching Expressions with Details

Exercise 2.5

Match expressions on the left with the appropriate details on the right.

a) In compliance with your instructions, ...

b) Concerning Article 17 governing vaccines, ...

c) With regard to the recent federal-provincial discussion, ...

d) With reference to Customs and Excise Directive D16-9, ...

_____ 1. ...the regulation expressly forbids additional issuances without a physician's order.

_____ 2. ...the quota system governing the importing of manufactured cotton sportswear will encourage Canadian production and employment.

_____ 3. ...all lighting fixtures in the warehouse have been changed to meet with the new Canadian Standards Association (CSA) regulations.

_____ 4. ...my main concern is that the demands of the provinces have not been fully considered.

Practising a Brief Memo

Exercise 2.6

Now write a complete beginning sentence for each of the three situations below. Use the *following up + confirming* pattern. Add any necessary details. Then use one of your beginning sentences to write a one-paragraph memo. Close with an expression of goodwill.

1. You wish to confirm that you are reserving a document which someone requested on the phone.

_____

_____

2. You wish to confirm that you are giving someone the authority to sign documents on your behalf.

_____

_____

3. You wish to confirm that a new date has been set for a meeting.

_____

_____

Your Own Response   **Exercise 2.7**

In this memo the head of a purchasing department has issued a blanket authorization to one of the purchasing agents. The head is now requesting information on submission dates of individual contracts in draft form.

Read the memo carefully and discuss it with members of the class. Then write a response to it. Show your completed memo to the teacher for comments and corrections.

Government of Canada Gouvernement du Canada	**MEMORANDUM NOTE DE SERVICE**

TO / A ▶ W.A. Rush Purchasing Agent	SECURITY · CLASSIFICATION · DE SÉCURITÉ
	OUR FILE – N / RÉFÉRENCE 2.7
FROM / DE Donald Boatner, Head Purchasing Department	YOUR FILE – V / RÉFÉRENCE
	DATE March 17, 1985

SUBJECT / OBJET   Recommendation and Authorization to Purchase

I have now approved and am returning to you the above-mentioned Recommendation and Authorization to Purchase for all implements.

The deadlines for final submission of purchase contracts are indicated on the front page of the authorization. Would you please indicate to me when I can expect to receive your individual draft contracts.

/mt   D. Boatner

Encl.
cc: C.L. Spratt

Writing a Responding Memo

Exercise 2.8

Respond to J. Morris' memo and request a change to the separate listing of senior support staff. Include appropriate opening and closing expressions. Discuss your memo with the teacher and share it with members of the class.

	Government Gouvernement **MEMORANDUM NOTE DE SERVICE**

Government of Canada / Gouvernement du Canada

MEMORANDUM   NOTE DE SERVICE

TO / A → A.L. McIntyre Senior Departmental Relations Officer	SECURITY · CLASSIFICATION · DE SÉCURITÉ
	OUR FILE – N / RÉFÉRENCE 2.8
FROM / DE J. Morris, Head Personnel Division	YOUR FILE – V / RÉFÉRENCE
	DATE 22 September 1986

SUBJECT / OBJET   Department Personnel Information Directory

As requested in your memo of 18 September 1986, enclosed is a complete listing of Departmental Senior Personnel Advisors and senior support staff.

Please note that advisors are listed by department, and support staff are listed separately. Please advise me immediately of any requests for further changes to the listings.

I hope this is to your satisfaction.

J. Morris
_____
J. Morris

BUYING TIME

Sometimes you cannot provide a complete response right away. It may be because you don't have sufficient information, because you are unsure of what your reaction will be, or because you want to wait for something else to happen before you react. In cases like these, you may want to "buy a little time".

Pinpointing Expressions   **Exercise 2.9**

Read the following sentences and underline the buying-time expressions.

1. With regard to your request for educational leave, we will be studying this request at the next Management Committee meeting and will inform you of our decision as soon as possible.
2. Your suggestion for a revised schedule has been placed on the agenda of the next meeting and will be given careful consideration.
3. I have written to three manufacturers for the information you requested and will forward their replies to you.
4. All submissions to the Transit Study Group will be considered before any final decisions are made.
5. We will let you know our reaction to the redevelopment plan as soon as the provincial government informs us of the status of the Millar property.
6. Corrective measures have been approved and will be undertaken as soon as the necessary budget credits are obtained.

Promising a Later Response   **Exercise 2.10**

You have received a request from the Western Regional Office for information on environmental clean-up procedures for dealing with chemical spills. A report on this subject is due for release next month. Acknowledge the request and promise to send a copy of the report as soon as it is available.

Exchange your finished memo with another student for comments.

Unit 3   The Informing Memo

All memos and letters are written with the purpose of informing the reader, but this unit deals specifically with those memos which contain such important information that writers draw attention to it in the first sentence through the use of informing expressions. These expressions, which are not normally a part of spoken English, are very common in administrative writing. In fact, informing memos rarely begin without them.

GIVING SIMPLE INFORMATION

A memo which is written to convey information to the reader usually begins with an introductory expression which signals the purpose of the memo. The most common expressions of this type are:

This is to inform you that ...	**Would you please note that ...**
For your information, ...	**This is to advise you that ...**
Please note that ...	**Please be advised that ...**

- The openers which use "inform(ation)" are usually used to introduce information of the fact or data kind.

- The openers which use "note" are usually used to introduce information which the writer intends the reader to remember for reference.

- The openers which use "advise(d)" are usually used to introduce information of the opinion or advice kind.

It is true that many writers use these expressions interchangeably with no great effect on the correctness of the memo. But for more precision the special meanings above should be observed.

Beginning Sentences   **Exercise 3.1**

Choose openers to begin the following sentences. Observe the three meaning suggestions.

1. _____ we have received the publication which you requested.

2. _____ the annual golf tournament will be held on June 28.

3. _____ there will be a fire drill today at 3:45.

4. _____ summer hours go into effect on Monday, July 5.

5. _____ Technitron will be giving a demonstration of new equipment tomorrow at 10:30 p.m. in Room 950.

6. _____ your new union steward is Jenny Eaton.

Completing a Short Informing Memo   **Exercise 3.2**

Short informing memos frequently follow this pattern:

Informing Sentence   +   Detail   +   Closing Remark

Use sentences 1, 2, and 3 from Exercise 3.1 as the opening sentences for three short informing memos. For each of the sentences, choose two appropriate sentences from those below to form a one-paragraph memo. Add your own details if you wish. Discuss your memo with your teacher and the class.

1. Your co-operation would be appreciated.

2. You may pick it up at your convenience at the library any time between 8:30 and 4:30.

3. We look forward to a repetition of last year's great success.

4. All those interested in participating should phone Lynn Clarey at 993-1573.

5. You are requested to leave the building as quickly as possible, using the staircase.

6. We are pleased to have been of service.

REQUESTS FOR ASSISTANCE

One of the memos in Exercise 3.2 ended with a request for assistance: "Your co-operation would be appreciated".

Here are some other endings of this type:

It would be appreciated if you could bring this to the attention of your staff.

Any additional comments would greatly assist me.

Your written approval would be welcome.

Your written comments would be helpful.

Any suggestions you might have would be greatly appreciated.

I would greatly appreciate any suggestions you might have.

I would welcome any additional comments.

Writing a Memo   **Exercise 3.3**

Write your own information memo for one of the two situations outlined below. Follow the *informing sentence* + *detail* + *closing remark* pattern. Exchange your memo with another student to get suggestions for improving it.

1. You: Administrative Services Officer

   Your readers: All staff

   Purpose: To inform the staff that they should not wear boots or overshoes into their offices but should leave them on the racks provided

2. You: Head of Division

   Your readers: Division staff

   Purpose: To announce that you will be taking education leave for a 6-month period and that one of the staff will be replacing you in your absence

MAKING AN ANNOUNCEMENT

Many memos are written to make announcements. Sometimes writers may want to begin
with a date; sometimes they may want to begin
with a person's or organization's name. Below
are five sentences which present information
in slightly different ways.

Combining Information

Exercise 3.4

Combine the expressions on the left with the information on the right.

a) Effective April 10, ...

b) Beginning (on) April 10, ...

c) On April 10 ...

d) April 10 ...

e) Starting at 11:00 a.m., ...

_____ 1. ... Mrs. R. Fletcher will assume the duties of Division Chief, International Trade.

_____ 2. ... marks the 25th anniversary of John Ferguson's service in this department.

_____ 3. ... Rosener and Thompkins, Management Consultants, will conduct an evaluation of the cost effectiveness of our operations.

_____ 4. ... there will be a meeting of the Joint Consultation Committee to discuss areas of mutual concern.

_____ 5. ... the steering committee discussed a full-length proposal for organization changes in the service.

Practising Informing Memos

Exercise 3.5

In Exercise 3.4 you wrote beginning sentences for informing memos. Now write a complete memo using the information in one of the following outlines.

Supply missing details before writing the memo.

1. Mrs. R. Fletcher:
     Past Experience
            3 years — Excise Division, Revenue Canada
            5 years — Foreign Investment Review Agency
            4 years — Department of Trade and Commerce
     Education
            M.B.A. — University of British Columbia
            P h . D . — University of Toronto
     Specializations
            • taxation and regulation
            • international trade law

2. Joint Consultation Committee:
     Purpose of Meeting
     Place
     Time
     Kinds of Suggestions Required

3. Rosener and Thomkins:
    Location
- 3rd floor, Room 101 and 102
- consultation, Room 300

    Information
- travel expense records
- requisition records
- out-of-town travel projections
- project proposals for 1986
- staff work schedules

    Procedures
- consultation with unit directors every two weeks
- consultation schedule to follow
- records to be submitted April 15

STATING A PURPOSE

Another way to begin an informing memo is by stating its purpose. Here are some examples:

The purpose of this memo is to ...   **This memo outlines ...**
The aim of this memo is to ...   **My purpose in writing ...**
This memo is to ...   **I am writing to inform you ...**

Practising Expressions   **Exercise 3.6**

Use the above expressions to state your purpose in the sentences below.

Example: *This memo outlines the Commission's guidelines on the reorganization of the Staff Development Branch.*

1. _____ that the department's policy on northern development will be reviewed during the next trimester.

2. _____ the main factors that were taken into consideration in the recent decision to abolish free parking privileges.

3. _____ is to suggest a number of directions which we might take in future and to stimulate discussion of these directions.

4. _____ inform you of the budget reporting schedules which will apply to all units in the department.

Reconstructing Sentences   **Exercise 3.7**

Each of the sentences in Exercise 3.6 can be written differently. If a different opening expression is chosen, a different grammatical construction may be required. Practise changing opening expressions and grammatical constructions.

1. Begin sentence 1 with:
The purpose of this memo is to _____

2. Begin sentence 2 with:
The aim of this memo is to _____

3. Begin sentence 3 with:
This memo outlines _____

4. Begin sentence 4 with:
This memo outlines _____

RECALLING

Recalling expressions are used at the beginning of informing memos a) when the reader already knows what the memo is about, or b) when it is polite to assume that the reader already knows what the memo is about. These expressions are listed in order of the degree of certainty on the part of the writer. The most certain are first; the least certain are last.

You are no doubt aware ...	**As you are aware, ...**	**As you may already know, ...**
As you know, ...	**As you may be aware, ...**	**You may recall ...**

Practising Expressions   Exercise 3.8

Match expressions a-e with sentence completions 1-5.

a) You may recall ...

b) You are no doubt aware ...

c) As you know, ...

d) As you may be aware, ...

e) As you may already know, ...

_____ 1. ... the Branch has been considering a reorganization for several months.

_____ 2. ... I first visited your installations in 1976.

_____ 3. ... we placed an order for 15 copies of the above-mentioned report on June 1.

_____ 4. ... there was a sharp increase in the cost of energy consumed per household.

_____ 5. ... that the deadline for submission of all proposals was last Friday.

Making Impressions on a Reader   Exercise 3.9

The recalling expressions in this exercise can convey a variety of attitudes on the part of the writer. Which impression does each of the following sentences convey to you? Compare your impressions with another student.

   a) annoyance   b) politeness   c) formal business

1. You are no doubt aware that we placed an order for 15 copies of the above-mentioned report on June 1.

2. You may recall that I first visited your installations in 1976.

3. As you know, the Branch has been considering a reorganization for some time now.

4. You are no doubt aware that the Minister has recently stated that the government wishes to do all it can to foster the development of the performing arts across the country.

5. As you know, all bicycles are to be left in the garage, not taken into individual offices.

6. You may recall that we first indicated our desire to be involved in a project of this type some three years ago.

7. As you know, the deadline for submission of all proposals was last Friday.

8. You are no doubt aware that there has been a sharp increase in the amount of energy consumed per household.

INDICATING UNDERSTANDING OF A PROBLEM

The expressions below reassure the reader that the writer knows about and understands some difficulty that exists. As such, these expressions serve a positive function. Nevertheless, they are also frequently used as a prelude to unpleasant information.

It has been drawn to my attention that ...   **It is my understanding that ...**

It has come to my attention that ...   **We recognize/appreciate that ...**

It is fully appreciated that ...   **I have recently been informed of ...**

It is recognized that ...   **I (can) realize/understand that ...**

It is understood that ...

Evaluating the Intent of Expressions   **Exercise 3.10**

Read the following sentences and decide whether these expressions serve a) only to reassure, or b) to reassure and to lead to some disagreeable information. Discuss with members of the class.

1. While I understand that this is only a minor matter, I would appreciate your rectifying the problem as soon as possible.

2. It is fully appreciated that you will not be able to complete the project before the end of the year.

3. We wish to congratulate you on your excellent efforts on our behalf. Please be assured that we recognize how difficult it is to please all of the people all of the time.

4. Though I realize that a memo has already been sent, I am afraid that another one will have to be issued immediately.

5. I can appreciate that many of you have previous commitments which cannot be altered, but a large turnout would be most appreciated.

6. I have recently been informed of your decision to increase the number of person years for our development unit.

7. Although I agreed with your original decision to relocate the training division to the Benson Building, it has come to my attention that the move will cause considerable liaison difficulties with our research unit.

8. It has been drawn to my attention that the field officers in your district have not as yet established boundary areas for applications for timber licenses.

REQUEST FOR ACTION (CLOSING)

Many memos end with a request. Some of the standard closing expressions listed below politely call for immediate action; some call for action by a specified date.

May we have your reaction at your earliest convenience.

We would appreciate hearing from you at your earliest convenience.

Would you kindly take action immediately.

I would appreciate your comments on the proposed form before May 1.

You are requested to submit your proposals by October 15.

Writing an Action Memo   **Exercise 3.11**

Write a complete memo using the following patterns. Show the final draft of your memo to your teacher for feedback.

Stating Purpose   +   Indicating Understanding   +   Request for Action

You: Unit Manager

Reader(s):   Office Supervisor(s)

Purpose: You have not received the usual monthly reports detailing your staff's compressed work week schedules. You have to report to the Area Manager on the effectiveness of these schedules in maintaining efficiency. Your report must be ready within a week.

POINTING OUT

In a memo of this type, the writer wishes to direct the attention of the reader to something that he or she should be aware of. In contrast to a simple informing memo, the writer here is merely referring to an existing document or situation which the reader may not know about. The pointing-out expression may be used at the beginning of a memo or in the middle, depending on the situation and the writer's preference.

Your attention is directed to ...   **I would like to direct your attention to ...**
You may be interested to note ...   **I would like to point out that ...**
It should be noted that ...   **Please note that ...**

At the beginning of a memo, a pointing-out expression may be preceded by a responding expression, as in this example.

In connection with your memo of October 3, your attention is directed to paragraph 15.09 of your Collective Agreement, which stipulates that a maximum of 26 weeks of maternity leave is to be granted to an employee. Additional leave is usually granted at the discretion of the local manager.

Combining Responding and Pointing-out Expressions   **Exercise 3.12**

One of the following sentences does not require expressions from both columns. Complete the sentences by selecting an expression from each of the columns; then decide which sentence does not need two.

RESPONDING EXPRESSIONS   POINTING-OUT EXPRESSIONS

In connection with ...   **please note that ...**
Further to ...   **your attention is directed to ...**
With regard to ...   **it should be noted that ...**
In response to ...   **I would like to point out that ...**
Concerning ...

1. _____ your request for the bilingual bonus, _____
   _____ Treasury Board Directive 294-1 for clarification of regulations governing the granting of bonuses.

2. _____ your question about the source of the statistics included in the Minister's report, _____ the statistics on mineral exports were quoted from the department's publication, which I have enclosed.

3. _____ your request for a completion date for next year's directory pages, _____ the preparation of these pages is a most time-consuming task. Therefore, our target date is delayed by three months to December 18.

4. _____ your request for copies of recent publications by Revenue Canada, _____ I am attaching two copies of our brochure "A History of Federal Sales and Excise Taxes".

5. _____ the appeal procedures for numbers 917 and 932, _____ grounds for appeal must first be fully established.

AVOIDING WORDINESS

It is important to use pointing-out expressions to draw the reader's attention to a document or situation. However, in order to avoid complicated or wordy style, the writer must be careful. Generally, pointing-out expressions can be omitted if the context of the situation is clear. And if two such expressions occur, one should be omitted.

Wordy: *With regard to the redeployment program, I would like to point out that it will be necessary for the department to provide a job description for each position.*

Better: *With regard to the redeployment program, it will be necessary for the department to provide a job description for each position.*

Wordy: *For your information, please note that your application will be reviewed by our staff along with the other 200 we have received.*

Better: *Please note that your application will be reviewed by our staff along with the other 200 we have received.*

Editing Pointing-out Expressions   **Exercise 3.13**

Read the following five sentences. Decide which sentences can be improved by editing out a pointing-out expression.

1. It should be noted that, as a result of the program, all personnel seconded to a department or agency will be the administrative responsibility of that department.

2. With reference to my budget proposal of February 3, 1985, I would like to direct your attention to Section D, page 14, and point out that clerical staff allotments are in excess of guidelines laid down by Treasury Board.

3. Your attention is directed to Section 14.2J(ii) of the Employment Act, which regulates appeal procedures in this type of staffing action.

4. I would like to point out that your attention is drawn to my memo of July 15, 1986, in which I outlined the changes in the regulations.

5. With regard to the request for additional support documents (my memo of September 9, 1985), it should be noted that the request was for documents only for the period January 1, 1984, to June 30, 1984.

EXPECTING/PREDICTING

A writer of memos is frequently required to make work-related predictions. The expressions listed below are part of the language normally used to signal a prediction or an assessment of a likely outcome. These expressions are used at any point in a memo where the writer wishes to make a prediction.

It is to be hoped that ...	**We anticipate that ...**
It is expected that ...	**We expect that ...**
It appears that ...	**We hope that ...**
... seems to indicate that ...	**We are confident that ...**

Completing Sentences   **Exercise 3.14**

Choose from the above expressions to complete the sentences. Discuss what you think the rest of the memo would have dealt with.

1. _____ wage and price controls will not affect our bargaining position for some time yet.

2. _____ relations with a number of foreign countries will continue to flourish in the next decade.

3. The continuing rise in unemployment _____ more drastic measures will be required on the part of governments.

4. _____ only a certain percentage of the members covered by this Collective Agreement will be satisfied with the terms that have been reached.

Practising an Informing Memo   **Exercise 3.15**

Write an informing memo to department supervisors informing them of a change of date, schedule, and speakers for a one-day training session. Diary page A shows the arrangements for the first plan; diary page B contains the new arrangements.

A.   Previously Announced   B.   New Arrangements

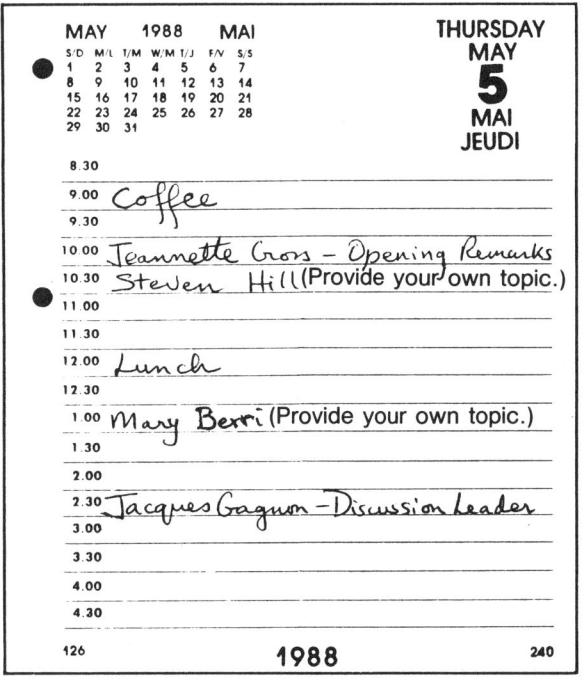

Unit 4   The Evaluating Memo

Besides conveying or confirming information, memos may also provide a vehicle for analysis or evaluation. There are a number of situations which require a writer to make evaluations. For instance, a policy paper or a report may arrive with a request for comments or criticism. The writer then writes an evaluating memo.

In this unit we look at analysis and criticism. Writing evaluations is an important part of government and business correspondence, and the evaluating memo requires careful wording to achieve an appropriate tone.

Positive Evaluation   **Exercise 4.1**

The following memo is an example of positive evaluation. The expressions and vocabulary convey much of the writer's positive tone. Read the memo and answer the questions that follow.

■✦ Government Gouvernement	**MEMORANDUM NOTE DE SERVICE**

Government of Canada   Gouvernement du Canada

MEMORANDUM   NOTE DE SERVICE

	SECURITY · CLASSIFICATION · DE SÉCURITÉ

TO / A ►   Ruth Bronson
             Graphics Section

OUR FILE – N / RÉFÉRENCE
4.1

FROM / DE   Jane Stevens
             Public Relations

YOUR FILE – V / RÉFÉRENCE

DATE
20 October 1986

SUBJECT / OBJET   FLIGHT SAFETY ILLUSTRATIONS

The photostats of your cartoon series concerning flight safety were circulated to selected individuals for consideration, in accordance with Steve Collins' letter of September 15.

The safety of aircraft operations is indeed a matter of utmost concern to the Department of Transport, especially in its role as overseer of personnel training. Your comprehensive series of cartoon illustrations is judged to be potentially highly useful in the publications of flying clubs and flying training schools in their programs to educate personnel in operations safety. While use of these illustrations by private groups is entirely optional, we are confident they will find the cartoons as valuable as we have.

I have taken the liberty of forwarding your excellent artwork to the following aviation associations:

Pro Flying Club   Provincial Owners and Pilots Association
Suite 607   2137 Marine Drive S.E.
1177 Booth Street   Vancouver, B.C.
Ottawa, Ontario   4V8 1T4

I wish you every success in your discussions with the above-mentioned associations.

Jane Stevens

TL/je
c.c. Steve Collins

---

1. The writer's positive evaluation is conveyed by the choice of words used to describe R. Bronson's illustrations. Find five positive descriptive words.

    a) _____   c) _____   e) _____

    b) _____   d) _____

2. The closing sentence uses a positive expression. What is that expression?

    _____

3. Why is the expression "I have taken the liberty of ..." likely to be understood by R. Bronson as a positive assessment of her illustrations?

4. Is the general tone of the memo formal and polite, or personal and enthusiastic?

Evaluating Positively   **Exercise 4.2**

Write a short memo (no more than three sentences) to your supervisor. Your memo will accompany and comment on a report prepared by someone in your section. The report studies various types of computers and recommends a particular model for purchase by the section. You agree with the recommendation.

Show your completed memo to the teacher for comments and corrections.

EXPRESSING CRITICISM (DISAPPOINTMENT)

Not all memos are positive, and on occasion we may want to be directly critical. In such a case we can use some of the following negative expressions. We should realize, however, that they are only useful if we want to be quite open about expressing annoyance or displeasure.

It does not seem possible to ...	**I regret that ...**
It is unfortunate that ...	**I am very disappointed with/that ...**
It is difficult to believe that ...	**I am sorry that ...**

A more tactful way of expressing criticism is to soften its impact with a positive introduction.

Too Blunt: *Your report fails to achieve its purpose.*

Direct: *It is unfortunate that your report does not achieve its purpose.*

Tactful: *While it is obvious that a great deal of thought has gone into the preparation of your report, it unfortunately falls short of its purpose.*

Writing Tactful Criticism   **Exercise 4.3**

Work in small groups or pairs for this exercise. Reword each of the following excessively blunt criticisms in two ways: a) as a direct criticism beginning with one of the negative expressions, and b) as a tactful criticism, beginning with a positive statement. For both a) and b), consider changing the vocabulary.

1. You have wasted a great deal of time compiling these figures; they do not give a complete picture of last year's expenditures.
2. Mr. Johnson does not have the capacity to work under pressure. Otherwise, he is a satisfactory employee.
3. Your unit seems incapable of handling the processing of the personnel files; we are sending Mr. Malt, who will see to it that you do it properly.
4. You simply have not understood my instructions for moving the telex machines. Contact Public Works immediately to arrange to move this equipment.

Reacting to a Situation   **Exercise 4.4**

How would you react to the following situations? Prepare a written response to one of the situations listed below. Exchange your response with another student and examine how outspoken you are. Check with the teacher.

1. You have just received a letter from head office stating that your request for additional staff has been refused. At present, your staff is voluntarily working through two lunch hours per week to correct finance errors from various other departments.
2. You have been asked to give written approval for something that you consider unjustifiable.
3. Information Services promised to send a transcript of an important speech to you. It is now a month since the speech was delivered and you have not received the transcript.

REFUSING

A refusal can easily be mistaken for criticism. This kind of memo demands that the writer use tact and diplomacy, yet still be honest and clear. To achieve this requires careful selection of vocabulary and expressions.

It is common practice to emphasize the positive before the negative, and then to re-establish a positive tone.

Positive   +   Negative   +   Positive

Refusing Tactfully   **Exercise 4.5**

The following memo is an example of tactful refusal.

■✴ Government **Gouvernement** **MEMORANDUM NOTE DE SERVICE**	
of Canada du Canada	

MEMORANDUM   NOTE DE SERVICE

SECURITY · CLASSIFICATION · DE SÉCURITÉ

TO
A   A.A. Smythe
      Director

OUR FILE – N / RÉFÉRENCE
      4.5

YOUR FILE – V / RÉFÉRENCE

FROM
DE   G.G. Snell
        Training Officer

DATE
      December 31, 1986

SUBJECT
OBJET   Mr. Frederick Osborne

Thank you for your memo of December 13 nominating the above-noted employee as a candidate for our training program commencing in March.

I regret very much that it is too late for me to accept this nomination. The deadline of December 1 for acceptance of nominations is necessary to allow time for the complete documentation of the nominees' files for review by the Selection Committee.

Should Mr. Osborne still be interested in a program for the term commencing in September, I would suggest that you submit a further letter of nomination on his behalf during the period March 30 to July 1. This will allow ample time for the documentation.

G.G. Snell
                                                        G.G. Snell

/zm

---

1. What is being refused in the memo?
2. What expressions make the memo tactful?
3. How does the writer conclude in a positive way?
4. What is the other purpose of the memo?
5. Could the memo be improved by adding a closing expression? If so, suggest one. If not, why not?

Writing Tactful Sentences **Exercise 4.6**

How would you tactfully reject the following requests? Write an introductory sentence or two only. Work alone and then exchange your sentences with another student.

REQUEST | REASON FOR REJECTION

1. An employee wishes to have one year of paid education leave to take a degree in Canadian history.

   Your director does not feel that Canadian history is directly relevant to the work done in your office.

2. The librarian has submitted a request for 25 additional journal subscriptions.

   You feel that you can justify the expense for only seven of these subscriptions.

3. Someone from another section wishes to second one of your employees for a six-month period.

   You feel your staff is already overworked and you cannot possibly manage with fewer employees.

4. The head of another department has asked you to organize a survey of the handling and storage of the department's records for the purpose of starting a feasibility study for converting to computer tape storage.

   You and your staff are overworked, and you do not have the time, the expertise, or the staff necessary to conduct such a difficult and detailed survey.

5. Someone has submitted a list of seven candidates to you for approval. The candidates are interested in attending a two-week training session in financial administration.

   You disapprove of four of the candidates on the list, and you feel that seven people are too many to send at one time for a full two weeks.

SUGGESTING A CHANGE

Tact and diplomacy are also important when suggesting a change. Again, it is usual to begin and end with positive comments so that the suggestion will not be seen as a criticism.

Suggesting Tactfully   **Exercise 4.7**

The choice of words and expressions is important in conveying a positive impression. In this memo, the first three paragraphs tactfully prepare the reader for the suggestion of change. Read the memo carefully before answering the questions.

1. Which word in the first paragraph conveys a positive impression of the draft?

    _____

2. Which expressions indicate that the writer does not wish to impose a) corrections or b) the suggested change?

    a) _____   b) _____

3. In the third paragraph, which positive words and expressions apply a) to the existing draft and b) to a possible series?

    a) _____   b) _____

        _____   _____

                                                 _____

4. The fourth paragraph contains two suggestions. Which one implies a criticism of T.C. Haynes' draft?

    _____

5. What effect does the other suggestion have?

    _____

6. Is the general tone of the memo formal and distant or formal but enthusiastic? Discuss.

    _____

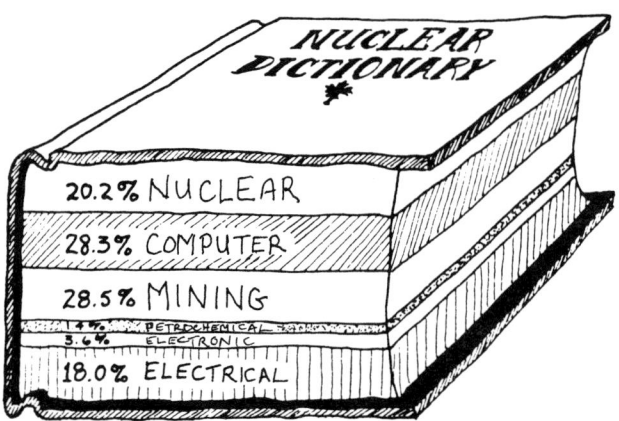

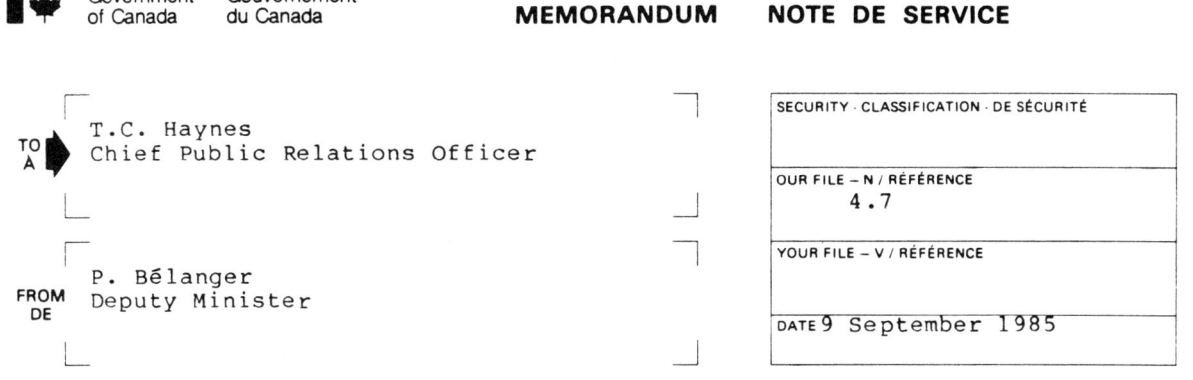

TO
A
T.C. Haynes
Chief Public Relations Officer

FROM
DE
P. Bélanger
Deputy Minister

SECURITY · CLASSIFICATION · DE SÉCURITÉ

OUR FILE – N / RÉFÉRENCE
4.7

YOUR FILE – V / RÉFÉRENCE

DATE 9 September 1985

SUBJECT
OBJET **Bilingual Technical Directory**

I have completed my editing of the very extensive draft bilingual
technical directory, which you forwarded to me for review last
June.

I have indicated my corrections in red pen; please feel free not
to accept them if you disagree with them.

On the whole, this lexicon is much more than a nuclear terms
dictionary. It comprises a large number of terms from the
computer, mining, petrochemical, electronic, and electrical
fields. The exhaustive number of terms does, indeed, form the
basis for many technical lexicons, which could well comprise a
thorough, up-to-date technical dictionary of Canadian terms. I
agree with you that such a series of dictionaries is a project
"devoutly to be wished".

I would suggest that we limit ourselves right now to strictly
nuclear terms and, at the same time, prepare a series of draft
proposals for a subsequent technical series.

Whatever you decide, please be assured of the continued support
of my department.

P. Bélanger

P. Bélanger

/we

GC 177   7540-21-798-8998

EXPRESSING SUGGESTIONS

The following expressions are often used to suggest a change. The large number of these expressions may be an indication of their importance in writing evaluating memos.

I would like to propose that ...
I would propose that ...
I am proposing that ...
I propose that ...

I would like to suggest that ...
I would suggest that ...
I am suggesting that ...
I suggest that ...

In my opinion ...
I think that ...
It seems to me that ...

Might
May
Could
Can
} **I/we suggest that ...?**

Would it be possible to ...?
Could we ...?
Should we ...?

I/We wonder whether
{ **you/we could ...**
you/we should ...
you/we might ...
you would ...

Making a Suggestion   **Exercise 4.8**

Two different situations follow. Choose one and write a complete memo. You may jot down initial ideas in point form in your draft, but write a full memo which suggests a change. Decide which expressions you will want to use before you begin writing.

1. You have been asked to prepare brief written comments on this floor plan. You feel it is inadequate for your needs, since you require at least three additional offices. Prepare your comments and suggest possible changes to the floor plan.

OFFICE FLOOR PLAN

1105	1104	1103	1102	1101
1106				
1107				
1108	1109	1110	1111	1112

2. You have been asked to prepare brief written comments on this proposal for grants. You are in agreement except for the grants to the Atlantic and Pacific regions which you think should be doubled. Provide reasons for your suggestion to increase these two grants.

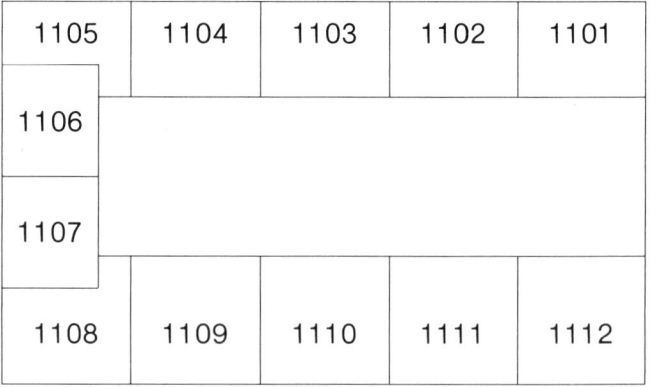

TRAINING PROGRAM

Region	Allocation
ATLANTIC	$195,000
QUÉBEC	$257,000
ONTARIO	$283,000
PRAIRIE	$283,000
PACIFIC	$187,000
CANADA TOTAL	$1,205,000

Evaluating a Memo Exercise 4.9

Read the following memo carefully and discuss the study questions with members of the class and with the teacher.

■✦ Government   Gouvernement   **MEMORANDUM   NOTE DE SERVICE**
of Canada   du Canada

TO ▶ **A**	Guy Normand Unit Chief
FROM **DE**	Joan Vincent Division Chief

SECURITY · CLASSIFICATION · DE SÉCURITÉ

OUR FILE – N / RÉFÉRENCE
4.9

YOUR FILE – V / RÉFÉRENCE

DATE January 28, 1986

SUBJECT
OBJET   INDIAN LIAISON OFFICER ANNUAL REPORTS

The volume and detail of your reports make any final analysis by this office or the Minister's Office difficult. Also, since the reaction to these reports must come from the regions, we propose a new procedure which should facilitate reading and monitoring them.

Future submissions should consist of the following:

a) the annual report itself;
b) a brief summary of the report's highlights;
c) regional reactions to the report;
d) a progress report on items unresolved or 'carried over' from the previous year; and
e) any general regional comments, for example, on the tenor of our relations with the provincial Indian Association.

Regarding points c) and d), you should keep in mind that, when the Minister visits Native Peoples' communities, he may be asked directly why progress is not being made on specific problems. These problems are likely 'carried over' points from previous reports. It would, therefore, be prudent for regions to keep a log of all Liaison Officer suggestions which should be reviewed, updated, and reported on as progress is made.

Joan Vincent
Joan Vincent

---

1. Identify four suggesting expressions in the memo.

2. How direct is the first sentence in the memo?
    Would the sentence annoy the reader?

3. Is the general tone of this memo formal and direct or formal with a personal touch?

4. What is the main suggestion the writer makes?

5. If you were to receive this memo, would you take the suggestions as items for consideration only or as steps to be implemented immediately?

Unit 5　　　　Editing Memos

An Editing Decision   Exercise 5.1

THE SUBJECT

1. Is the subject line clearly worded?
2. Does it relate clearly to the content of the memo?

LOGIC

1. Paragraph 1 says that the writer's purpose is to congratulate Jean Smith on her efforts. Is this misleading? What is the purpose of the memo?
2. In paragraph 2, the writer says "Although unfortunately". This is awkward. How would you correct it?
3. In paragraph 2, the writer says the employee's work should be related to the education leave requested. Is this relationship logical? How would you rewrite it?
4. Is it necessary to invite comments on a rejection of a request?

GRAMMAR AND STYLE

1. In paragraph 1, choose a better word for "effort".
2. In paragraph 2, the article in the first sentence is incorrect. Correct it.
3. In paragraph 2, the writer says "not very much related". Correct this.

TONE

1. What is the general tone of the memo? Is it polite and neutral, or is it rude?
2. The closing paragraph sounds paternalistic. How would you encourage Jean Smith to continue her education?

A FINAL STEP

Rewrite the memo. Make the purpose clear and adjust the words and phrases so that the tone is polite and neutral, yet encouraging.

Government Gouvernement
of Canada du Canada

MEMORANDUM   NOTE DE SERVICE

TO
À

Jean Smith
Records Section

FROM
DE

Monica Laws
Division Head

SECURITY · CLASSIFICATION · DE SÉCURITÉ

OUR FILE – N / RÉFÉRENCE
5.1

YOUR FILE – V / RÉFÉRENCE

DATE
December 19, 1987

SUBJECT
OBJET

Education Leave Request

In response to your request for one year of paid education
leave to take a degree in Canadian history, I would like
to congratulate you on your effort for higher education.

Although unfortunately, I must remind you of the policy
of the department in this matter. In order for such a
leave to be granted, the employee's work must be directly
related to the type of education requested. As you are
aware, a degree in Canadian history is not very much
related to your work.

Your interest in education is fully appreciated. I would
appreciate your comments.

Monica Laws

Monica Laws

ML/dd

GC 177   7540-21-798-8998

An Editing Decision   **Exercise 5.2**

THE SUBJECT

1. Is the subject line clearly worded?
2. Does it relate clearly to the content of the memo?

LOGIC

1. What is the purpose of the memo?
2. In paragraph 4, the writer says "... information on the above ..." What does "above" refer to? Is the reference clear?

GRAMMAR AND STYLE

1. In paragraph 1, choose a different word in the expression "have to inform". Would it be better to express some regret at conveying the bad news?
2. In paragraph 1, the pronoun "I" is used. In paragraph 2, the pronoun "we" is used. Decide which pronoun is better and make the pronouns consistent (parallel) throughout the memo.
3. In paragraph 2, the writer says "we feel that". Is "we feel" accurate? How would you change the wording?
4. In paragraph 3, repair the tense of "could". Omit "gain advantage to ..." Omit the word "Furthermore". Is the sentence clearer?

TONE

1. Is the general tone of the memo appropriate?

A COMPARISON

1. Compare the two original education leave memos (5.1 and 5.2).
2. Which memo is better? Justify your decision.
    Which one is more grammatical; which one is more organized and logical; which one has a more appropriate tone?

A FINAL STEP

Rewrite the memo and make the changes discussed. Are other changes necessary?

I✦ Government   Gouvernement
of Canada   du Canada

MEMORANDUM   NOTE DE SERVICE

SECURITY · CLASSIFICATION · DE SÉCURITÉ	
OUR FILE – N / RÉFÉRENCE 5.2	
YOUR FILE – V / RÉFÉRENCE	
DATE 7 Feb. 1984	

**TO
A** W. Davidson
Records Section

**FROM
DE** T. Cianci
Career Planning

**SUBJECT
OBJET** Request for Paid Education Leave

In response to your request for one year of paid education leave to take a degree in Canadian history, I have to inform you that we cannot authorize this leave.

While we appreciate your desire to improve your knowledge, we feel that Canadian history is not directly related to your present position and to the goals of this organization. The Personnel Administration Act, Article 26, is very specific and states that "paid education leave must be granted only when the required training is directly related to the job or would facilitate promotion of an employee."

I am aware of your great interest in history, and I would like to point out that you could gain advantage to apply for leave without pay. Furthermore, this branch offers financial help for employees who take evening courses.

If you need additional information on the above, do not hesitate to contact me at any time.

T. Cianci
T. Cianci

GC 177   7540-21-798-8998

An Editing Decision   Exercise 5.3

THE SUBJECT

1. Is the subject line clearly worded?
2. Does it relate clearly to the content of the memo?
    Is the memo about the "punch-in" system, about creating better incentives, or about increasing productivity?

LOGIC

1. In paragraph 2, what does "a tighter control" refer to?
2. In paragraph 2, what does "to accomplish this" refer to? Does it refer to "a tighter control" or to increasing productivity?
3. Is the purpose of this memo to make a suggestion?
    If so, what is the suggestion?

GRAMMAR AND STYLE

1. Is the article necessary in "a tighter control"?
2. Is the article necessary in "the employees"?
3. Is "we (the supervisors)" clear? Who wants to have the meeting?
4. In paragraph 2, correct "is adopted".

TONE

1. Is the general tone of the memo personal and direct, formal and polite, or neutral?
2. Is the expression "honestly do not think" necessary?
3. Is the expression "I personally feel" necessary?
4. The writer says "I feel". Does he mean "I think"? Which expression is better? Why?

A FINAL STEP
Rewrite the memo and correct the errors in grammar and the defects in tone.

	Government	Gouvernement	**MEMORANDUM**	**NOTE DE SERVICE**

TO
À

L. Lavoie
Chief of Operations

FROM
DE

C. Burns
Supervisor

SECURITY · CLASSIFICATION · DE SÉCURITÉ
OUR FILE – N / RÉFÉRENCE
5.3
YOUR FILE – V / RÉFÉRENCE
DATE
9 May 1985

SUBJECT
OBJET   Comments on the "Punch-in" System

This is further to your memo dated April 10, 1985, in which
you proposed that employees adopt the "punch-in" system.

I fully agree with you that we must increase productivity and
that we would have a tighter control if the "punch-in" system
is adopted. However, I honestly do not think that adopting
a tighter control would increase productivity. I personally
think that, to accomplish this, we should give the employees
more incentives to work faster. I feel that if we (the supervisors) could meet with you, we could discuss different possibilities to create such incentiveness.

Your consideration of this suggestion would be appreciated.

C. Burns
C. Burns

GC 177   7540-21-798-8998

An Editing Decision   **Exercise 5.4**

THE SUBJECT

1.   Is the subject line clearly worded?
2.   Does it relate clearly to the content of the memo? Which working area is referred to? Should this information be included?

LOGIC

1.   Does it seem reasonable to suggest a floor plan that was submitted one year ago as a solution to a present problem? How would you handle the suggestion?
2.   What is the purpose of the memo?

GRAMMAR AND STYLE

1.   In paragraph 2, the pronoun "you" is used twice. What tone does this convey? Reword the sentence.
2.   In paragraph 2, the word "since" could be confused with "because". How would you correct this?
3.   In paragraph 2, the verb tense is incorrect. Correct it.
4.   In the closing sentence, the article is used incorrectly. Correct it.

TONE

1.   In paragraph 2, "You might not realize ..." sounds abrupt and condemning. Choose a more polite opening expression.
2.   In paragraph 3, "I would like you to consider ..." sounds too abrupt. Choose a more polite and neutral expression.
3.   The closing sentence is too abrupt. Reword the sentence to make it more polite and neutral.

 A FINAL STEP

Rewrite the memo. Try to adjust the wording so that the tone is polite and tactful, yet still conveys a complaint and a reasonable suggestion.

I✦ Government Gouvernement
of Canada du Canada

MEMORANDUM   NOTE DE SERVICE

TO
À E. Ehemic
   Office Manager

FROM
DE L. Bander
    Executive Assistant

SECURITY · CLASSIFICATION · DE SÉCURITÉ	
OUR FILE – N / RÉFÉRENCE 5.4	
YOUR FILE – V / RÉFÉRENCE	
DATE March 7, 1985	

SUBJECT
OBJET **NOISE LEVELS IN OUR WORKING AREA**

        I would like to draw your attention to the noise in our
working area.

        Since you have hired the new employees the noise in this
section has become intolerable. You might not realize that the
area is too small to accommodate so many people.

        I would like you to consider the floor plan I submitted
to you last year. It may be a solution to the present situation.

        It will be appreciated if you take an action as soon as
possible.

L. Bander

L. Bander

GC 177   7540-21-798-8998

An Editing Decision   **Exercise 5.5**

THE SUBJECT

1. Is the subject line clearly written?

2. Does it relate clearly to the content of the memo?

3. Does the wording of the subject line suggest that the purpose of the memo is a request for serials subscriptions?

LOGIC

1. When was the request for 25 subscriptions made? Should the date of the request be included in the memo?

2. In paragraph 2, the connector "in spite of" is incorrect. Choose another connector, so that the logical connection in the paragraph is correct.

3. In paragraph 3, the first sentence sounds like an apology. Is it appropriate to make an apology? Try combining paragraph 3 with paragraph 2.

GRAMMAR AND STYLE

1. In paragraph 3, the second sentence is a conditional. The auxiliaries are not parallel. Correct them.

TONE

1. Is the tone of the closing sentence paternalistic, or is it polite and formal?

2. Suggest a more polite and neutral closing expression.

A FINAL STEP

Rewrite the memo and make the changes discussed. Does your finished version require further changes?

Government   Gouvernement   **MEMORANDUM   NOTE DE SERVICE**
of Canada   du Canada

TO **A**	Donna Greig Acquisitions Librarian
FROM **DE**	Dan Lentz Documents Librarian

SECURITY · CLASSIFICATION · DE SÉCURITÉ

OUR FILE – N / RÉFÉRENCE
5.5

YOUR FILE – V / RÉFÉRENCE

DATE   86/05/15

SUBJECT
OBJET   Request for Serials Subscriptions

I acknowledge receipt of your request for twenty-five additional serials subscriptions.

In spite of the efforts spent lately to improve the quality of our services, we cannot justify the expense for more than seven of the titles submitted.

It was a difficult decision considering your requirements in this area. Should the budget be increased, I would gladly reconsider your request.

I know you will find good use for these new publications.

D. Lentz
Dan Lentz

GC 177   7540-21-798-8998

An Editing Decision   Exercise 5.6

THE SUBJECT

1.   Is the subject line clearly worded?
2.   Does it relate clearly to the content of the memo?

LOGIC

1.   Paragraph 2 is unfocused. Why can't the writer accept late submissions?

GRAMMAR AND STYLE

1.   In paragraph 1, the although clause is misplaced. Who made the "recent request"? When? Whose overtime schedules? Rewrite the sentence.
2.   In paragraph 2, correct the punctuation in sentence 2.

TONE

1.   Is this a complaint memo, a request memo, or both?
2.   Is the tone of this memo formal and polite or rude and abrupt?
3.   Think of a better opening expression for "Should I remind you that ...".
4.   The closing sentence is far too abrupt. Reword it.

A FINAL STEP

Rewrite the memo so that the logic in paragraph 2 is clear and the general tone is more polite.

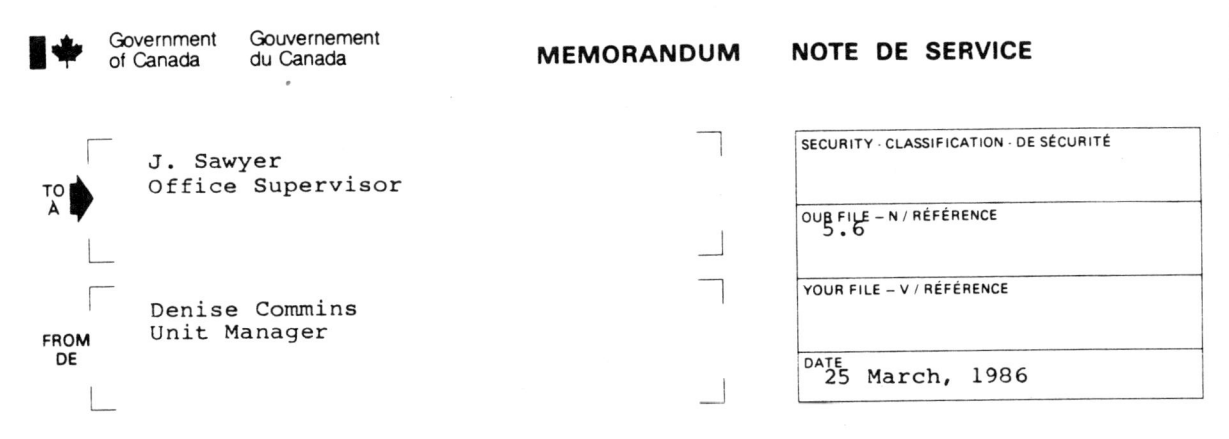

TO
A

J. Sawyer
Office Supervisor

FROM
DE

Denise Commins
Unit Manager

SECURITY · CLASSIFICATION · DE SÉCURITÉ

OUR FILE – N / RÉFÉRENCE
5.6

YOUR FILE – V / RÉFÉRENCE

DATE
25 March, 1986

SUBJECT
OBJET   **Overtime Schedules**

Although a recent request, I still have not received all
overtime schedules for this month.

Should I remind you that these schedules are due on the first
Friday of every month so that I can include them on the
month-end budget. As you know, any overtime must be approved
in advance otherwise no payment is allowed. I cannot accept
any late submission.

Would you then take immediate action.

Denise Commins

Denise Commins

GC 177   7540-21-798-8998

An Editing Decision   **Exercise 5.7**

THE SUBJECT

1. Is the subject line clearly worded?

2. Does it relate clearly to the content of the memo? Does the memo only comment on a floor plan or does it criticize and suggest a specific change?

LOGIC

1. What was the main purpose for the writer's request to move?

2. What two rooms were omitted from the floor plan?

3. How should this information be stated in the memo? Where should it be stated?

4. In paragraph 4, the writer says "that floor". Which floor does she mean?

5. In paragraph 4, "another place" is not clear. What other place does she mean? Correct the sentence.

GRAMMAR AND STYLE

1. In paragraph 1, the writer attempts to be positive. She says "very elaborate and well done". The choice of words does not sound very positive. Think of another choice of words.

2. In paragraph 2, the writer says "I feel". The memo says she has studied an elaborate floor plan. Does she mean "I feel" or "I think"? Which expression is better?

3. In paragraph 3, the pronoun "it" does not have a referent. Rewrite the sentence.

TONE

1. Does the last sentence (paragraph 5) sound formal and positive, or does it sound direct and impolite? Choose another expression that is more appropriate.

A FINAL STEP

Rewrite the memo so that the purpose is clear. Choose different words and expressions in order to make the general tone more positive.

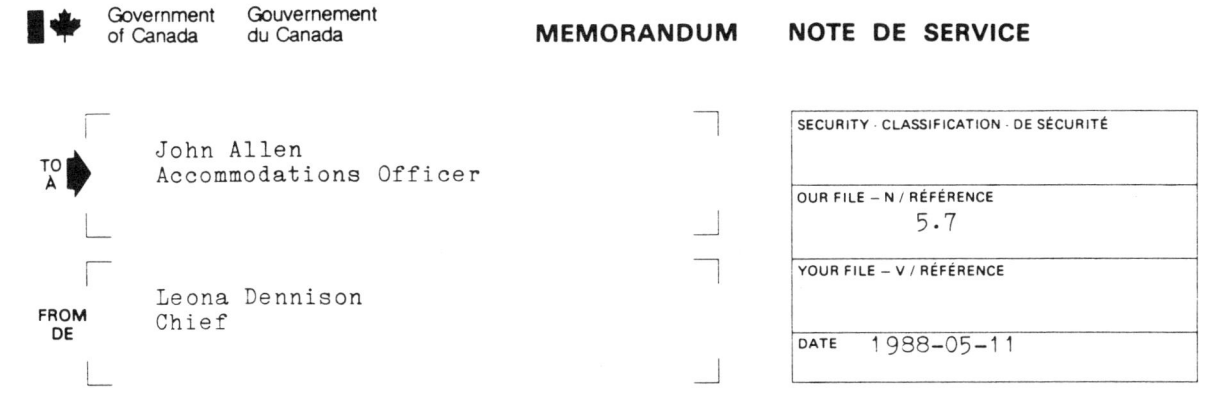

MEMORANDUM   **NOTE DE SERVICE**

Government   Gouvernement
of Canada   du Canada

TO
À

John Allen
Accommodations Officer

FROM
DE

Leona Dennison
Chief

SECURITY · CLASSIFICATION · DE SÉCURITÉ

OUR FILE – N / RÉFÉRENCE
5.7

YOUR FILE – V / RÉFÉRENCE

DATE   1988-05-11

SUBJECT
OBJET

COMMENTS ON YOUR FLOOR PLAN

The draft of the floor plan that you prepared and submitted is
very elaborate and well done. I can only say that you have
worked very hard on it.

However, I feel that the space allotted for my division is
inadequate for my needs. You have left no space for a
boardroom nor for an interview room, which is badly needed.

I can appreciate the difficulties that it will cause you in
trying to replan all this, but obtaining space for these
purposes was the main reason for my request to move.

I propose that 1) you try to obtain more room on that floor,
or 2) you look for another place.

I expect to hear from you on this matter in the near future.

L. Dennison
Leona Dennison

GC 177   7540-21-798-8998

Writing Role-Play   **Exercise 5.8**

Here are five situations that provide information for the writer and the receiver in an exchange of memos. Work in pairs and select as many as you wish to work on. Decide the purpose of the memo you will write. Exchange your final copies and discuss the reasons for your reactions.

Produce a final copy that would be suitable for actual circulation.

UNION REPRESENTATIVE

You were requested at a union meeting to approach management with specific and serious complaints about the ventilation system in your building. You know from having worked for five years in the department that the bad air in all seasons causes discomfort, illness, and absenteeism. Write to the director about the complaints. Suggest that he or she arrange for the Health and Safety Branch to test the air in the building and monitor it over a period of time. You wish to be formal, polite, and yet firm because you are the representative of the employees.

DIRECTOR

You have, in the past three years, attempted to move Public Works to correct the ventilation problem in the building. You have not been successful. Yet you agree with the staff that there is a problem. You are not certain, however, that the problem is as serious as people say it is. You are worried about calling in Health and Safety Branch because such an action might endanger your efforts to deal with Public Works. Judge the merits of the union memo and decide upon a response. You have always had good relations with the union, and you do not wish to damage those relations. Inform the union representative of your course of action.

CR-05 EMPLOYEE

This year you have strong personal reasons for wanting to take your two-week vacation in October. You know that this is a busy time when holiday leave is not normally granted. However, you have always taken your leave in the usual summer months during the six years you have been in the unit. You feel that your reasons are valid. Write a memo to your unit head and inform her or him of your situation and request the October leave.

UNIT HEAD

You are aware of the heavy work load expected in October and of the difficulties in allocating one employee's responsibilities to an already overworked staff. However, you know that the CR-05 has been a responsible and dependable employee who has never before made special requests. Judge the memo on its merits and respond with a memo which either informs the employee of your acceptance of the request or politely rejects it.

A REMINDER

1. Indicate the English titles of individuals precisely.
2. State the subject line clearly and accurately.
3. Relate the contents of the memo directly to the subject line.
4. Use an appropriate closing.
5. Use vocabulary and tone appropriate for the individuals to whom you are writing and for your message.
6. In a long memo, vary your grammatical constructions to improve your style.

TRAINING CO-ORDINATOR
You have been asked to make room arrangements for a half-day seminar at the Conference Centre. The seminar is for 25 Division Chiefs from various departments. Write a memo to the director of the Conference Centre making arrangements for space, tables, audio-visual equipment, and refreshments.

CONFERENCE CENTRE DIRECTOR
You have received a Treasury Board directive that all un-necessary expenditures by your facility be reduced. You feel that half-day seminars could be arranged more inexpensively in other facilities in a department. Write a response which informs the co-ordinator of the new directive, and suggest an alternative.

CLACK!
CLICK!

PURCHASING AGENT
You are one of five purchasing agents in the unit. All of you are required, because of lack of staff, to type your own let-ters and contracts in a standard format on typewriters. Write a memo to the purchasing manager explaining the benefits of purchasing an office computer to make this time-consuming chore more efficient. Justify the expense and request the pur-chase of a computer.

PURCHASING MANAGER
As manager of the purchasing unit you are very aware of budget constraints. Yet you know that your agents could do their work more efficiently if the more ordinary chores were made easier. Judge the memo you receive and write a response which either rejects the request or accepts it.

WORD PROCESSING OPERATOR

You are one of ten operators in a typing/word-processing pool. Your room is crowded and has only two windows. Four out of the ten operators smoke continually during work hours. You, as a non-smoker, are bothered by the smoke in the room. You feel the smokers are inconsiderate and, in a sense, unprofessional. Write a memo to the work supervisor of the pool. Complain about the situation and suggest several reasonable remedies. You do not wish to cause an unfriendly atmosphere in the room, but you do want some changes made.

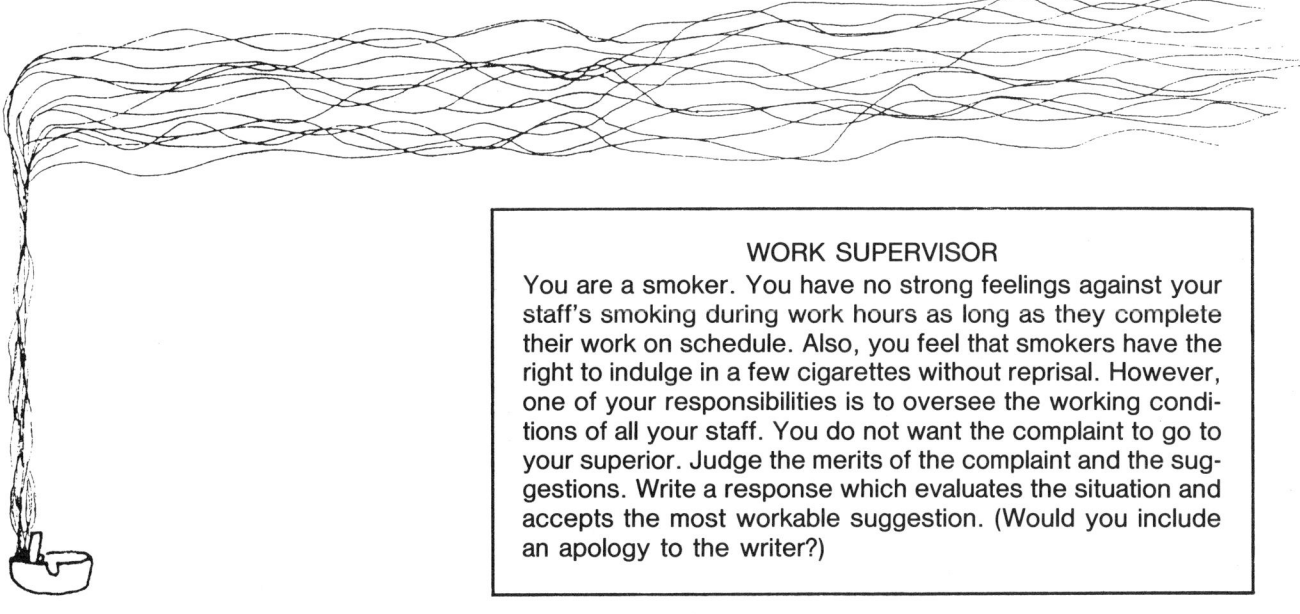

WORK SUPERVISOR

You are a smoker. You have no strong feelings against your staff's smoking during work hours as long as they complete their work on schedule. Also, you feel that smokers have the right to indulge in a few cigarettes without reprisal. However, one of your responsibilities is to oversee the working conditions of all your staff. You do not want the complaint to go to your superior. Judge the merits of the complaint and the suggestions. Write a response which evaluates the situation and accepts the most workable suggestion. (Would you include an apology to the writer?)

PART TWO

LETTERS

Letters are primarily used for communication with the public, but they may also be used for formal communication within a department or between departments.

Letters by public servants are normally formal and polite in tone. However, this is not equally true in industry, where the trend is toward greater informality in both format and tone.

Unit 1   Parts of a Letter

FORMAT

1. Letterhead
2. Inside address
3. Attention line (optional)
4. Date
5. Salutation
6. Reference (rare in letters)
7. Complimentary closing
8. Signature, title, and address
9. Reference initials
10. Enclosures
11. Copies

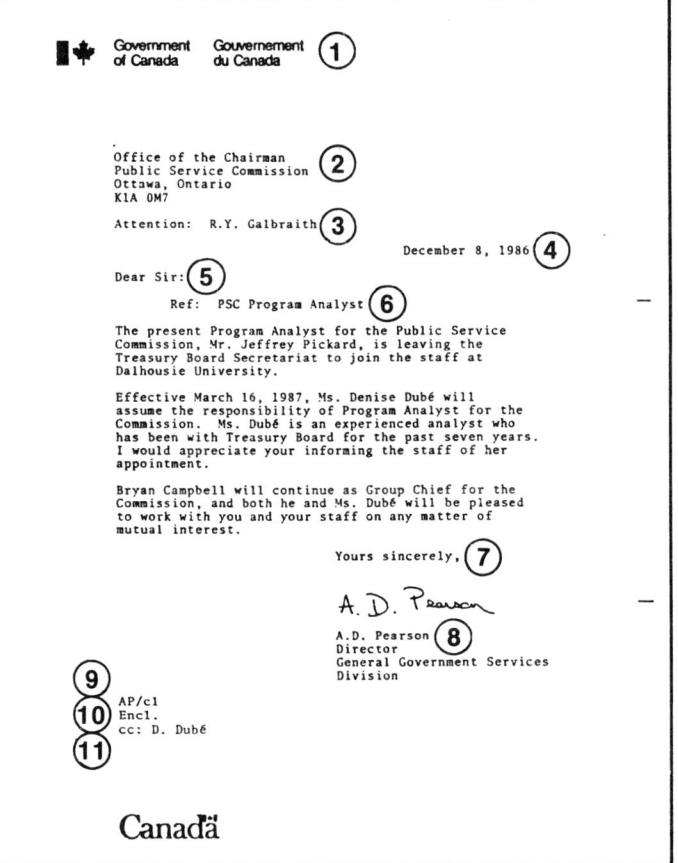

1. Letterhead

Most departments in the public service now use a standardized letterhead that includes the name of the department or agency. The writer's address is normally placed at the end of the letter after his or her name and position title, not after the letterhead.

2. Inside Address

This is usually aligned with the left-hand margin. Open punctuation (no punctuation at the end of lines) is most common.

3. Attention Line

This is not common in government correspondence, since letters are usually addressed directly to individuals rather than to departments. However, when a letter is sent to a department, but an individual is cited, the person's name is generally placed between the address and the salutation, using one of the following:

   Attn.:   Att.:   Attention:

The attention line is often placed on the envelope in the lower left corner.

4. Date

In letters the date is usually written out in full in one of the following ways:

   September 1, 1987   1 September 1987

5. Salutation

The salutation is followed by a colon (:), or sometimes a comma (,).

6. Reference Line

The use of the reference line has been borrowed from the subject line in memos but is rare in letters. If a reference line is used, it is indicated:

   Re: Ref:

7. Complimentary Closing

"Yours truly" and "Yours sincerely" are the most common closings.

8. Signature, Title, and Address

The signature is usually followed by the title of the sender. The address of the sender is often shown below the title.

9. Reference Initials

As with memos, reference initials provide a record of who wrote the letter and who typed it.

10. Enclosures

If there are any enclosures, this is usually indicated below the reference initials.

11. Copies

If copies of a letter are being sent to someone, this is usually indicated in the same way as it is in memos. (See page 5.)

Another abbreviation occasionally used is b.c., which stands for "blind cover". It is not used on the original copy and appears only on one copy, which is privately sent to a specially concerned party without the primary recipient's knowledge.

SALUTATIONS

Letters directed to specific individuals commonly use a personal salutation.

Dear Ms. Watkins: **Dear Mrs. Parker:**

Dear Mr. Lang: **Dear C. Thomas:**

In exceptionally formal letters, a man is addressed as "Dear Sir" and a woman as "Dear Madam". In a letter directed to a business or an unknown person, the salutations "Gentlemen" or "Dear Sirs" are sometimes used. Other possibilities are:

Dear Sir/Madam: **Dear Sir or Madam:**

Dear Madam:
Dear Sir:

The salutation is sometimes followed by a comma (,), but more often by a colon (:).

COMPLIMENTARY CLOSINGS

These are the most commonly used complimentary closings.

Yours truly,   **Sincerely yours,**

Yours sincerely,   **Cordially,**

For certain formal letters, such as those sent to Ministers, Deputy Ministers, Executive Directors, and Directors General, it is customary to end:

Yours respectfully,   **Respectfully,**

ADDRESSES

The following sample address illustrates the most common format. Note that there is no punctuation at the ends of the lines, except for periods necessary with abbreviations. The postal code can also be placed two or three spaces after the province.

French and English Addresses   **Exercise 1.1**

French conventions of address writing differ from English conventions.

L. Ostman	L. Ostman
Marketing Officer	Agent de commercialisation
Canadian Fiddlehead Corporation	Office canadien des têtes de violon
Gesner Building, Room 237	Édifice Gesner, pièce 237
155 St. Louis Blvd. W.	155 ouest, boul. St-Louis
Moncton, N.B.	Moncton (N.-B.)
E1H 3Y9	E1H 3Y9

In this example, what are the differences?

1. Punctuation _____

_____

_____

2. Capitalization _____

_____

_____

Abbreviating Names of Provinces

Exercise 1.2

Supply the usual abbreviations for Canada's provinces and territories. Check your answers with the teacher.

1. Newfoundland _____
2. Labrador _____
3. Prince Edward Island _____
4. Nova Scotia _____
5. New Brunswick _____
6. Quebec _____
7. Ontario _____
8. Manitoba _____
9. Saskatchewan _____
10. Alberta _____
11. British Columbia _____
12. The Northwest Territories _____
13. The Yukon Territory _____

Expanding Abbreviations

Exercise 1.3

Here are some abbreviations often used in addresses. What are the full forms?

1. Ave. _____
2. Blvd. _____
3. Dr. _____
4. St. _____
5. Pl. _____
6. Sq. _____
7. Cres. _____
8. Rd. _____
9. Pkwy. _____
10. Ct. _____
11. U.S. _____
12. G.B. _____
13. R.R. _____
14. P.O. _____
15. E. _____
16. W. _____
17. N. _____
18. S. _____
19. N.E. _____
20. N.W. _____
21. S.E. _____
22. S.W. _____
23. Ste. _____
24. Apt. _____
25. Rm. _____
26. Bldg. _____

Abbreviating Addresses

Exercise 1.4

In each of the following addresses, select the words that can be abbreviated and substitute the correct abbreviation. Discuss your answers with the teacher.

1. D. Marsh, Chairperson
   AETL Association
   2013 Milne Drive Southwest
   Calgary, Alberta
   T2H 2H5

2. M. Davies
   Post Office Box 53
   Rural Route 3
   Old Orchard Crescent
   Penticton, British Columbia
   V2A 6R5

3. J. Cruikshank, Head
   Research and Development
   Saskatchewan Development Corporation
   231 Third Avenue North, Suite 706
   Saskatoon, Saskatchewan
   S0G 4N0

4. P. Green, Manager
   Grainpak Limited
   1269 Bruce Boulevard
   Lethbridge, Alberta
   T1H 4T8

5. Royal Canadian Mounted Police
   "C" Division
   Post Office Box 559
   4225 Dorchester Boulevard West
   Westmount, Quebec
   H3Z 1V5
   Attention: C. Campbell

6. G. Brodeur
   Northern Canada Power Commission
   301 Federal Building
   Whitehorse, The Yukon Territory
   Y1A 1Y9

7. G. L. Mayer, Chief
   Technical and Production Service
   Central Publishing Division
   Transport Canada Training Institute
   Post Office Box 3330
   Cornwall, Ontario
   K6H 6L2

8. Mr. R. B. MacDonald, Manager
   Micrographics Unit
   Records Management Division
   Canadian Coast Guard College
   Mariner Building, Room 45
   156 Coast Road
   Sydney, Nova Scotia
   B1P 1C0

9. J. Lombard, Chief
   Field Operations
   Polar Continental Shelf Project
   Energy, Mines and Resources Canada
   Federal Building
   Tuktoyaktuk
   The Northwest Territories
   X0E 1C0

10. M. Sussex, Consultant
    Department of Consumer Relations
    Souris Building, Room 444
    76 Richmond Road
    Winnipeg, Manitoba
    R2M 4V7

Memo or Letter   **Exercise 1.5**

The administrative letter is usually used instead of a memorandum when the writer is corresponding with a person outside the department or outside the federal government. In some departments, a letter may be used internally when a greater degree of formality is required.

Would a memo or a letter be more suitable in the following situations?

		MEMO	LETTER
1.	Making an offer of employment to a candidate in a recent competition	☐	☐
2.	Thanking a member of the public for suggesting the polar bear as a national emblem for Canada	☐	☐
3.	Informing the staff that there will be a lunch-hour showing of a film on fire prevention	☐	☐
4.	Informing unit employees of possibilities of transfer to Vancouver and Winnipeg	☐	☐
5.	Informing someone that your department does not hire directly because all staffing actions go through the Public Service Commission	☐	☐
6.	Internal report on a one-day seminar	☐	☐
7.	Announcing the beginning of summer hours	☐	☐
8.	Explaining the procedure for obtaining Canadian landed immigrant status to a U.S. citizen	☐	☐
9.	Thanking a foreign expert for being a plenary speaker at a national conference	☐	☐
10.	Requesting that all correspondence received by your department be answered within ten days	☐	☐

Matching Expressions with Purpose   **Exercise 1.6**

The following exercise contains excerpts from administrative letters. The excerpts contain expressions which show the writer's purpose. Match each of the excerpts with one of the purposes listed here.

  a) Acknowledging
  b) Requesting
  c) Apologizing
  d) Thanking
  e) Informing

1. _____ For the present, you are requested to submit only one copy of any submissions for program approval.

2. _____ It would be appreciated if we could have a target date for the publication of your report.

3. _____ I regret that it was not possible to inform you of these requirements sufficiently in advance to permit scheduling of this meeting; the Task Force recommendations have just become known.

4. _____ Thank you for your recent letters outlining your views on the variety and quality of products which should be available to Canadian consumers.

5. _____ I am writing to inform you of EECL's intention to place a contract with your University for the development of heat cycle machines.

6. _____ I wish to explain that it is the department's expectation that only three vessels will be constructed on the basis of the plans developed under this contract.

7. _____ We wish to apologize for shipping old mailing labels, for which you had to pay return postage.

8. _____ I regret to have to convey this information to you, but I see no alternative.

9. _____ I would be pleased to have your opinion on the legal position of AETC regarding the accident.

10. _____ As requested by Joanne Wright, I am sending you an outline of the demonstration given by our consumer consultant.

11. _____ Thank you for your interest in this proposal.

12. _____ For your information, the department has, to date, refused three separate requests from the industry for an extension of protective tariffs.

13. _____ Please be advised that it is necessary to provide two copies of reports to the Research Board in the Maritimes Region.

14. _____ Enclosed are duplicate copies of schedules of the Air Navigation Orders submitted to you for clearance.

15. _____ In response to your enquiry of 20 January, I am happy to supply you with information regarding the new Road and Motor Vehicle Traffic Safety Office.

Unit 2   The Beginning Sentence

Review of Beginning Sentences   Exercise 2.1

The beginning expressions in the following exercise are similar to those presented in Part One. Match the expressions below with the completions.

a) This is to inform you that ...

b) I am writing with regard to ...

c) As you may recall, ...

d) I am writing this letter in order to ...

e) Attached is ...

_____ 1. ... last November we discussed the possibility of a lateral transfer to enable me to gain managerial experience.

_____ 2. ... the three-day symposium for all AS-06's that will take place in Montebello, Québec, January 18-21.

_____ 3. ... your identification card, which will enable you as non-military staff to gain access to this building at all times.

_____ 4. ... because of recent restrictions on hiring, no department expansion is anticipated.

_____ 5. ... request submissions for topics for discussion at our next regular interdepartmental meeting.

Unscrambling Sentences   Exercise 2.2

Unscramble and punctuate each of the sentences.

1. On October 18 / order / firm / subscription / one-year / a / your / placed / we / an / with / for

_____

_____

2. our / Bureau's / indicated / in the / of May 9 / the / areas / following / encourage / I / discussions / during / As / I / participation

_____

_____

3. ensure / copies / requisitions / that / to / are / Mrs. Mackay / all / Please / of / sent

_____

_____

4. acknowledge receipt of / requesting / travel / Deputy Ministers / 1980 / since / and / international / letter / This will / information / by Ministers / your / on

_____

_____

5. Please / subject to / policy changes will be implemented / the following / be advised that / Cabinet Document 1982-CCT-0641

_____

_____

ACKNOWLEDGING RECEIPT OF CORRESPONDENCE

How do you let someone know that you have received a piece of correspondence? Here are some of the expressions most commonly used for this purpose.

This is to acknowledge receipt of ...　　　　**I refer to your letter of ...**
Further to your letter of ...　　　　　　　　**I am in receipt of ...**
With regard to your letter of ...　　　　　　**We have received ...**
In reply to your letter of ...　　　　　　　　**Thank you for ...**
I am acknowledging receipt of ...

From the Filing Cabinet　　　　　　　　　　　　　　　　**Exercise 2.3**

From your office, bring a letter in which you acknowledged receipt of a piece of correspondence. Copy your letter and distribute it to the class.

Discuss the following points.

OPENING EXPRESSIONS

Are they appropriate for the person receiving the letter? Look for other expressions that could be used.

TONE

Is the tone too formal, too direct, or too personal for the situation or for the person receiving the letter?

GRAMMAR

Is the grammar correct and consistent? Is its organization clear?

SPELLING AND PUNCTUATION

Are there any spelling errors? Is the punctuation correct?

Writing an Acknowledging Letter　　　　　　　　　　　**Exercise 2.4**

Here are some situations which call for letters introduced by the expressions listed above. Choose one and write an appropriate letter. Exchange with another student for discussion.

1. You are a staffing officer, and you have just received 200 applications for a recently advertised position.

    *   Indicate to each applicant that you have received her or his application.
    *   Say that you will be in touch shortly regarding interviews.

2. You are an executive secretary. Your office has announced a call for tenders for repairs to a government building.

    *   Acknowledge receipt of a bid.
    *   Inform the company that the bid has been submitted to the finance department for screening.
    *   Assure the writer that you will be in touch shortly.

3. You are in charge of correspondence in a competition for Canadian short-stories. As a result of an advertisement which was carried in all major Canadian newspapers, you have received over 500 manuscripts. However, you cannot accept manuscripts over a 20-page limit.

    *   Acknowledge receipt of a manuscript of 35 pages.
    *   Express regret that the manuscript is over the 20-page limit.

ACKNOWLEDGING FOR SOMEONE ELSE

Correspondence is often routinely delegated. How does an employee indicate he or she is answering for someone else? Here are some common opening expressions.

> **Your letter of ... has been passed to me for reply.**
> **... has requested that I reply to ...**
> **... has asked me to reply to ...**
> **On behalf of ...**
> **I have been asked to reply to ...**

Adding Details to Expressions   Exercise 2.5

Use these expressions to write complete opening sentences. Supply names, dates, and other information. Check your sentences with your teacher.

Example: *I have been asked to reply to your letter of February 18, 1986, in which you requested further details on staff allotment for the next fiscal year.*

1. _____

2. _____

3. _____

4. _____

Practising Expressions   Exercise 2.6

Read the following letter and fill in the blanks, using the expressions on the left.

I am enclosing

has asked me to reply to

regarding

I hope that

please do not hesitate

I regret that

should you require

Dear Mr. Davidson:

Mr. Franklin Smith _____ your letter of April 2 _____ your interest in the manufacture of oil and air filters for automobiles.

There are eleven companies in Canada manufacturing oil and air filters. _____ a page from the export statistics compiled by Statistics Canada. Unfortunately, filters are not accounted for separately in the statistics. _____ I do not have the means of determining the quantity or value of our exports of filters.

_____ this information is of some value to you. _____ any further information, _____ to write again.

THANKING

Here are some examples of how to express gratitude for something special.

We would like to take this opportunity to tell you how much we appreciate ...

May I take this opportunity to express my ...

We would like to thank you for ...

Thank you for ...

Details of what the writer is thanking someone for follow these beginnings. This type of letter often ends with a restatement of the initial thanking.

Practising Thanking Openers
Exercise 2.7

Write a complete thanking letter to one of the following:

1. A colleague in another city who has just sent you a letter of congratulations on your promotion

2. A university professor who was a guest speaker at a meeting that you organized

3. A specialist in another department who recently completed a comprehensive report under great time pressure

REQUESTING INFORMATION

These expressions are used to request information.

I would appreciate it if you could provide me/us with information on ...

I am writing for information on ...

I would like to have some information on ...

I am writing to enquire about ...

I understand that you have some information on ...

It has come to my attention that you may ...

I have recently heard that ...

Writing a Request
Exercise 2.8

Write a letter to one of the following individuals who have submitted reports to your department and request more information. Make the purpose of your request clear. Exchange your letter with another student for comments. Check with the teacher.

1. To: a management consultant in Supply and Services Canada
   For: specific recommendations to increase cost efficiency in your department

2. To: a Member of Parliament
   For: information on acid rain effects in her or his riding

3. To: the author of an article commissioned by Museums Canada
   For: information on the history of the Acadians

4. To: a staffing consultant
   For: details of a program to increase participation of Native Peoples in government

GOOD NEWS

Here are some ways of beginning a good news letter.

It is with great pleasure that I am able to inform you that ...
I take great pleasure in informing you that ...
It is my pleasant task to inform you of ...
It gives me pleasure to inform you that ...
I am pleased to inform you that ...

The following are more neutral but may be used for good news announcements.

This is to inform you that ...   **This is to confirm ...**   **Please be advised that ...**

Writing Good News Beginnings   **Exercise 2.9**

Write your own good news beginnings for the answers to the following applications.

1. Request for education leave (12 months, 75% of salary)

    _____

    _____

2. Participation in a competition for the design of a new public building

    _____

    _____

3. Request for a $10,000 grant to study the effects of the construction of high-rise apartment buildings in residential neighbourhoods

    _____

    _____

CONGRATULATING

Here are some common beginnings used to extend congratulations.

It is my pleasant task to congratulate you on ...
I would like to extend my sincere congratulations on ...
I would like to congratulate you on ...
I was delighted to hear that ...

Writing Congratulating Sentences   **Exercise 2.10**

Use the congratulating expressions from the list to introduce the following sentences.

1. _____
    you have been promoted to Director General.

2. _____
    your appointment to the Senate.

3. _____
    your 35 years of devoted service.

4. _____
    the completion and publication of your invaluable report.

BAD NEWS

Letters which convey bad news tend to be more indirect. They often begin with an informing or acknowledging expression and usually introduce the bad news with an expression of regret.

Unfortunately, I have to inform you that ...
We regret to inform you that ...
We regret that ...

Conveying Bad News **Exercise 2.11**

Read the following letter. What tone is established? What else might the writer have said to soften the bad news?

 Government   Gouvernement
of Canada   du Canada

Your file   Votre référence

Our file   Notre référence

2.11

A.R. Williams
483 Hatt Street
Keswick, Ont.
L4P 2L5

September 10, 1987

Dear Mr. Williams:

This refers to your application for Chief, Technical Services.

I regret to inform you that you did not meet the basic requirements for this position. However, we appreciate your interest in the competition and would like to take this opportunity to wish you every success in your career.

Yours sincerely,

R. Cheung

R. Cheung
Personnel Officer

/rf

Writing a Bad News Letter **Exercise 2.12**

Choose one of the situations in Exercise 2.9 and write a complete bad news letter. State the bad news tactfully and soften the impact through the use of an encouraging statement. Exchange your work with another student and check it with the teacher.

Making the Negative Polite Exercise 2.13

In the following sentences, there are negative words and undertones. First identify the negative elements; then rewrite the sentences to make them more tactful or at least neutral. Discuss your sentences with the teacher.

1. We cannot fill your order until the beginning of the month.
2. You must realize that we have to charge you for repairing the equipment, as the one-year guarantee has lapsed.
3. Since the deadline is January 26, a prompt reply is required.
4. We would have answered you sooner if you had not sent your letter to the wrong office.
5. Because you did not submit a complete dossier, your request for education leave has been denied.
6. The committee feels there are so many negative considerations that we should cancel this contract.

COMPLAINTS

Here are some common ways of beginning a statement of complaint. These beginnings are all extremely direct and are an immediate signal to the reader that the writer is angry or annoyed.

> **Please regard this as a formal complaint about ...**
> **I am writing to complain about ...**
> **I am writing with regard to a situation which I feel should not continue.**
> **I think you should know about ...**
> **I think you should be aware of ...**
> **We believe you have not ...**
> **I fail to see how ...**
> **We are somewhat at a loss to see how ...**

There are more indirect and neutral ways to begin a letter of complaint. It is common to begin with a pointing-out expression and then to state the complaint. Which approach you choose depends on the person to whom you are writing, your personality, and how strongly you feel about the issue. Here are some pointing-out expressions that help to set an indirect tone.

> **Your attention is directed to ...**
> **You will be interested to note ...**
> **I would like to draw your attention to ...**

Writing a Letter of Complaint Exercise 2.14

Choose a situation from the list below and write a complete letter of complaint. Decide if you will use the direct approach or the indirect approach. Supply all necessary details. Discuss your finished letter with another student and the teacher and get any suggestions for improvement.

1. Complain to a photocopier company about an excessive number of repairs to your office photocopier in the first year of use.
2. Complain to the building manager about the fluctuating temperature in your office.
3. Complain to a textile manufacturer in Hong Kong who has not submitted the required statistics on yearly exports to Canada.
4. Complain to a printing company about the poor printing of a report.

APOLOGIZING

Mistakes happen. When a writer is apologizing for a mistake, a number of common expressions may be used. The writer must decide whether it is better to apologize at the beginning of the letter, at the end, or both.

Deciding Where to Apologize   Exercise 2.15

Read through the following apologizing expressions and decide whether they would most likely be used at the beginning or near the end of a letter.

		BEGINNING	END
1.	I would like to apologize for ...	☐	☐
2.	I wish to apologize for ...	☐	☐
3.	... regret any inconvenience ...	☐	☐
4.	Once again, may I offer my sincere apologies ...	☐	☐
5.	I am sorry for ...	☐	☐
6.	I have been asked to convey sincere apologies ...	☐	☐
7.	Once again, I am sincerely sorry for ...	☐	☐

Writing a Letter of Apology   Exercise 2.16

Use one of the expressions in Exercise 2.15 to begin a letter of apology to a member of the public. Provide your own details or use one of the four suggestions below. Use another apologizing expression to close the letter. Exchange your finished letter with another student and get any suggestions for improvement.

1. It has taken you six weeks to answer a letter.
2. You sent incorrect information to a member of the public.
3. You have lost the documents submitted in support of an application.
4. A letter was sent to the wrong person by the mailroom and has finally been passed on to you.

Acknowledging
Apologizing
Buying Time
Complaining
Congratulating
Conveying Bad News
Conveying Good News
Criticizing
Expecting
Expressing Goodwill
Informing
Predicting
Recalling
Refusing/Rejecting
Regretting
Requesting
Suggesting
Thanking
Urging

Unit 3   Strategies

A good writer plans and organizes carefully. He or she may use strategies such as recalling, thanking, apologizing, and notifying. The choice of the expressions used to implement these strategies combines with the overall plan to express the purpose of the letter and set its tone.

Reviewing Pointing-out Expressions

Match the segments on the left with those on the right.

a)   Your attention ...   _____   1.   ... be interested in ...

b)   You may ...   _____   2.   ... be wise to ...

c)   It might ...   _____   3.   ... is directed to ...

d)   I would like ...   _____   4.   ... to draw your attention to ...

Pointing Out in a Paragraph

Incorporate the following details into complete sentences, using one of the expressions in Exercise 3.1 at the beginning of every sentence. Then choose one sentence and write the entire first paragraph of a letter, adding all necessary details. Exchange your finished paragraph and get suggestions for improvement.

Example: *... Article 15 of the Collective Agreement ...*

Sentence: *Your attention is directed to Article 15 of the Collective Agreement for your group, which sets out in detail the conditions of leave without pay.*

1.   ... the revised insulation standards ...

_____

_____

_____

2.   ... the Deputy Minister has approved ...

_____

_____

_____

3.   ... our recent publication ...

_____

_____

_____

4.   ... the report of the regional transportation committee ...

_____

_____

_____

REVIEW OF EXPECTING AND PREDICTING

These expressions are used to signal a prediction.

It is to be hoped that ...	**We expect ...**
It is anticipated that ...	**We anticipate ...**
It is expected that ...	**... seems to indicate that ...**
It appears that ...	**It seems that ...**

SUGGESTING

After stating a prediction or expectation, writers often follow up with a suggestion. The following expressions are often used to introduce a suggested course of action. (See also page 34.)

It would be advisable to ...	**I might suggest/recommend ...**
It is recommended that ...	**I would advise ...**
It is suggested that ...	**I recommend/advise ...**
It may be useful to ...	**It might be wise ...**
You might consider it worthwhile ...	

Completing Sentences with Expressions

Exercise 3.3

Use expecting/predicting or suggesting expressions to complete these sentences. Check your answers with the teacher.

1. _____ we improve our planning procedures.

2. _____ that, with improved planning, we will be able to alleviate the pressures experienced in past years.

3. _____ you to examine these amounts and revise them if necessary.

4. _____ complete current projects before embarking on new ones.

5. _____ the reports will be released to participating agencies as quickly as possible.

Implementing Strategies

Exercise 3.4

A consulting firm has submitted a report proposing the establishment of a wildlife research station at a particular site. However, the site is near a small airport. Air traffic in the vicinity will probably increase considerably in the next five years. Write a letter suggesting that the consultants re-examine one of the other sites that have been considered. Use the following strategies:

Acknowledging   +   Informing   +   Expecting / Predicting   +   Suggesting

Regretting

On occasion, you may not be able to be of assistance to someone who has written to you. Read the letter to Mrs. Proctor to see how someone else in this situation has responded.

 Government   Gouvernement
of Canada   du Canada

Your file   Votre reference

Our file   Notre reference
3.4

April 28, 1986

Mrs. Louise Proctor
1407 Haida Street
Apt. 304
Nelson, British Columbia
V1L 3H4

Dear Mrs. Proctor:

This acknowledges your letter of April 4, in which you made enquiries about a position calling for experience in commercial art.

Unfortunately, the work of this office is connected with the promotion of industrial design and entails specialities which call for many years of experience in environmental, engineering, or industrial design.

We do not rule out the possibility that your talents may be in demand somewhere else in government. With this in mind, may we suggest that you write the Public Service Commission in Ottawa, outlining in detail your education, experience, and interests. We are enclosing an application form for this purpose.

May I take this opportunity to thank you for your interest in a government career and wish you every success in your application.

Yours sincerely,

G. Patry

G. Patry
Staffing Officer

GP/mg

Canadä

STUDY QUESTIONS

To gain an understanding of what makes this letter polite, read it carefully and answer the following questions. Discuss your answers with your teacher and the class.

1. What purpose does the writer accomplish in each paragraph?
2. Why could the letter not begin with the second paragraph?
3. Is the last paragraph essential? Why was it included?
4. How would Mrs. Proctor have felt if the second paragraph had started, "We suggest you restrict your applications to positions which call for the kind of experience you are able to offer"?

Practising Some Strategies   **Exercise 3.6**

Write a letter in which you follow these strategies. Use one of the situations given below or choose one from your experience.

Acknowledging +	**Regretting / Helpful Information / Suggesting** +	**Thanking**
Paragraph 1	Paragraph 2	Paragraph 3

1. You are unable to mail a copy of your latest annual report to a professor at a Canadian university as he or she has requested. You enclose a copy of last year's report instead.
2. You are unable to accept an invitation by a private firm to attend a one-day seminar on financial management. You suggest your executive assistant instead.
3. You have no authority to implement an excellent suggestion from a member of the public for improved service. You promise, however, to bring her or his suggestion up at the next management committee meeting and to forward the letter to someone in a more senior position.

URGING

These expressions are similar to suggesting expressions, except that they are more insistent.

> **I strongly urge ...**
> **I urge you to ...**
> **We would urge you to ...**
> **In this case, I would strongly suggest that ...**
> **I don't wish to pressure you, but ...**
> **I would emphasize ...**

Detecting Urgency   **Exercise 3.7**

Find and underline the words that express urgency.

1. Would you take steps to make your payments promptly on a monthly basis.
2. Your co-operation is anticipated.
3. It is expected that all members of the staff will attend this important meeting.
4. There is an urgent need for a labour relations conference within the next six months.
5. I strongly urge that such a conference be held within the next three months.
6. Your quarterly report is urgently requested.

Examining a Complaint Letter   **Exercise 3.8**

Here is an example of an indirect approach to a letter of complaint. Read the letter and discuss the questions.

 Government   Gouvernement
of Canada   du Canada

Your file   Votre reference

Our file   Notre reference
3.1

July 15, 1989

Dryden Equipment Supply
29 Maple Hill Road
Regina, Sask.
S4S 4C9

Dear Sir/Madam:

Your attention is directed to my letter of May 18, in which
I requested that you mail me your catalogue for 1989. With
my letter I enclosed a cheque for $10.00 as requested in
the advertising flyer. It is now July 15, and I still have
not received the catalogue.

Would you kindly mail a catalogue to me immediately. If
you are unable to do so, I will expect to have the cheque
returned to my office by August 1.

Yours truly,

E. Chow
Purchasing Manager

DISCUSSION QUESTIONS

1. What is the pointing-out expression in the letter? What other expressions could be used?
2. Is the tone of the request sentence impolite, or is it direct and straightforward?
3. What choices of words make the last sentence quite direct?
4. In your opinion, does the tone of the letter convey a very real complaint? Why or why not?

Determining Strategies   **Exercise 3.9**

 Government   Gouvernement
of Canada   du Canada

Your file   Votre reference

Our file   Notre reference
3.9

June 16, 1988

Jean N. Rossi
Personnel Manager
Richards Investment Corp.
726 Burret St.
St. John's, Nfld.
A1A 2B7

Dear Madam:

Mr. Robert Wellesley, who was formerly a pay clerk in
your firm, has given us your name as a reference.

We would appreciate a letter from you in which you
comment on Mr. Wellesley's capabilities, reliability,
and overall effectiveness while he was in your employ.

We will, of course, keep this information in the
strictest confidence. We are grateful for your
assistance in this matter.

Yours truly,

W. Dempsey

W. Dempsey
Staffing Services

/EB

DISCUSSION QUESTIONS

1. a) What strategies are used in this letter?
    b) Which expressions in the letter correspond to these strategies?

2. Is the general tone of this letter abrupt and rude, neutral, or formal? Discuss your decision.

3. In which paragraph is the main purpose of the letter stated?

Determining Strategies   **Exercise 3.10**

 Government   Gouvernement
of Canada   du Canada

You· ne   votre reterence

Ou· ne   Notre reterence
3.10

December 16, 1985

J.H. Sterling, Chairman
Finance Section
Dept. of Natural Resources
203 Farley Blvd.
Toronto, Ont. M4Y 3T4

Dear Sir:

There seems to be a lack of liaison between your
section and Mr. Jameson in the establishment of salary
procedures and information.

Your future assistance in improving communication
would be greatly appreciated, as it would expedite
Mr. Jameson's work and benefit the employees and the
department.

Yours truly,

N.J. Lorne
Director, Personnel Division

DISCUSSION QUESTIONS

1. a) What strategies are used in this letter?
    b) Which expressions in the letter correspond to these strategies?
2. What is the tone of this letter?
3. What is the effect of the briefness of the letter?
4. Suggest a closing paragraph which could make the letter more polite.

Determining Strategies   **Exercise 3.11**

 Government   Gouvernement
of Canada   du Canada

April 5, 1987   Your file   Votre reference

                                                Our file   Notre reference
                                                    3.11

T.B. Firth, Manager
The Canadian Salmon Fishermen's Assoc.
1789 University Ave.
Montreal, P.Q. H4X 3M9

Dear Sir,

        This will acknowledge your letter of March 28, in
which you requested information on the catch of Atlantic
and Pacific salmon in 1986.

        I regret that the final figures for the 1986 catches
are not available to us at this time, but these data are
being compiled by our Conservation and Protection Service.
I am bringing your letter to the attention of Mr. Snider,
Director of the Conservation and Protection Service, with
the request that he forward the statistics to you as soon
as possible. I estimate that the figures should be
complete by the end of July.

        I apologize for any inconvenience this delay might
cause you.

Yours very truly,

M. Steeles

M.M. Steeles, Director
International Fisheries Service.

/jm

DISCUSSION QUESTIONS

1. a) What strategies are used in this letter?
    b) Which expressions in the letter correspond to these strategies?

2. Is the polite formal tone of this letter appropriate?

Determining Strategies   **Exercise 3.12**

 Government   Gouvernement
of Canada   du Canada

Your file   Votre reference

Our file   Notre reference

November 23, 1988   3.12

Ms. Ruth N. Redley
Perfect Carpets Inc.
424 Leonard St.
Belleville, Ontario
K8P 1G4

Dear Ms. Redley:

You will remember that I wrote to you on November 5 and
telephoned you on November 15, asking if you would
forward to Statistics Canada the information they need in
order to give us a total compilation for Canadian factory
shipments of broadloom carpets for the year 1986.
Statistics Canada tells me that they have not yet
received your information.

I am writing to ask you again if you would forward the
required data to them. We are in difficulty because of
the lack of information we need.

Yours very truly,

J. Chiu

J. Chiu
International Economic Relations

DISCUSSION QUESTIONS

1. a) What strategies are used in this letter?
    b) Which expressions in the letter correspond to these strategies?
2. What is the general tone of this letter?
3. Is the tone appropriate?

Determining Strategies **Exercise 3.13**

 Government   Gouvernement
of Canada   du Canada

Your file   Votre référence

Our file   Notre référence
3.13

December 9, 1988

Miss K. Peters
44 Riverbend Rd.
Winnipeg, Manitoba   R2M 0Z4

Dear Miss Peters:

I have been asked to reply to your letter of
December 1 requesting information about the Department of
Finance for your high school's model parliament.

I am enclosing a copy of a summary of the department's
organization, the Minister's supplementary budget speech of
November 21, a press summary of the budget speech, and a
copy of a speech by the Minister on April 3. The latter
describes clearly how a budget is prepared.

I would suggest that your question about foreign
policy be directed to the Information Office of the
Department of External Affairs.

Yours sincerely,

A. Webb
Information Officer

Encl.

AW/KJ

DISCUSSION QUESTIONS

1. a) What strategies are used in this letter?
    b) Which expressions in the letter correspond to these strategies?
2. Is the general tone of this letter formal or friendly?
3. How appropriate is the tone?
4. Would a closing sentence be appropriate? If so, suggest one.

Unit 4   The Closing Sentence

The closings in this unit are useful both in letters and in memos. While memos often have no closing sentence, it is rare to end a letter without one.

THANKING

There are two main types of thanking closing: general thanking and specific thanking. The general thanking closing is often a mere formality; a specific thanking closing refers to a particular situation and may set a more personal and sincere tone.

General thanking closings:

> **Your co-operation is appreciated.**
> **We appreciate your co-operation.**
> **Thank you for your continued support.**
> **Thank you for your co-operation.**
> **Thank you for your interest in ...**

Specific thanking closings:

> **May I take this opportunity to thank you for ...**
> **May I thank you, once again, for giving me the opportunity to ...**
> **I wish to thank you for ...**

Concluding with a Thank You   **Exercise 4.1**

Decide which of the two letters needs a thanking closing. Choose one.

Dear Jack,

Thank you very much for your letter of March 15 inviting me to give a presentation at your annual meeting.

Unfortunately, I have a previous commitment on that day and will therefore not be able to attend.

_____

_____

_____

Dear Mr. Sawchuk:

The Area Supervisor, Manitoba Region, has brought to my attention your co-operation with him in completing the recent report on the cultivation of cereal grains in your area.

The department appreciates your help and involvement in this work. You have made an important contribution to the accuracy and completeness of the report.

_____

_____

_____

INVITING A REPLY

Inviting the reader to respond to your letter is a common way to close. These invitations are polite and neutral but invite a prompt reply.

> **Would you please let me have your comments at your earliest convenience.**
> **If ... suitable, would you kindly let us know.**
> **An early reply would be helpful.**
> **We look forward to ...**

Selecting a Closing | Exercise 4.2

Read the following letter and select a suitable closing.

Dear Sir:

In reference to our earlier discussions, I have compiled the more significant reactions to the Organization and Staffing Report; I am enclosing a copy of my summary for your information.

We have not as yet been able to update the report; however, we should be able to accommodate any reasonable request by your organization for current information.

You may also be able to get up-to-date information from Data Stream. This department would be pleased to assist you to access the Data Stream System.

_____

_____

SUGGESTING SOMEONE ELSE

You may wish to suggest that a more qualified person deal with a particular problem or request. Here are some common expressions.

> **Questions relating to ... should be directed to ...**
> **The staff there would be pleased to assist you.**
> **If you have any further questions, ... would be the best person to help you.**
> **In future, direct all questions of this type to ...**
> **Please direct all enquiries to ...**
> **You might get in touch with ...**

Predicting Effect on the Reader | Exercise 4.3

How would you as a reader react to the expressions? Discuss your answers.

1. a) Which of these expressions is likely to offend the reader?

    _____

    b) How would you modify this expression to make it less abrupt?

    _____

2. Which of these expressions does not guarantee that the person suggested can help?

    _____

3. Which of these expressions implies that the writer has already contacted the person suggested?

    _____

OFFERING FURTHER ASSISTANCE

The following endings are very common in letters and in memos. They serve to end a letter on a polite and helpful note.

Should you have any questions feel free to contact me at ...

Please do not hesitate to write if you require additional information.

If you have any other questions, please get in touch with ...

If you require further assistance, please do not hesitate to write ...

If you require further information, we would be most pleased to supply it.

Ending with an Offer of Help　　　　　　　　　　　　　　　　**Exercise 4.4**

Complete the following letter by using one of the endings from the above list.

Dear Ms. Llewellyn:

Thank you for your letter of September 3. I am enclosing a copy of our publication *Log Cabins You Can Build Yourself.* I hope this will answer the questions you asked in your letter.

_____

_____

CLOSING WITH AN EXPRESSION OF GOODWILL

The following expressions are used to end a letter with a note of goodwill.

I trust this will be to your satisfaction.

I trust that these arrangements meet with your approval.

I hope that this information will be of some assistance to you.

I hope that this is to your satisfaction.

Expressing Goodwill　　　　　　　　　　　　　　　　　　**Exercise 4.5**

Complete the following letter with one of the endings from the above list.

Dear Mr. Whyte:

We are pleased that you have accepted the invitation to give the keynote address at our upcoming conference. We are very much looking forward to what will certainly be an informative and interesting speech.

The usual stipend for this kind of address is $200. In addition, travel, accommodation, and meals and incidentals will be reimbursed upon presentation of receipts.

_____

_____

Sincerely,

Unscrambling Closing Sentences   **Exercise 4.6**

Unscramble each of the sentences. Provide capital letters and punctuation where necessary.

1.   receiving / i would appreciate / on the proposed form / before may 1 / your comments

_____

_____

2.   this delay / once again / has caused / i regret / any inconvenience

_____

_____

3.   with them / our understanding of the issues / i will get in touch / so that we can improve

_____

_____

4.   i would appreciate / by the end / hearing from you / of april

_____

_____

5.   your attending / to this matter / i would appreciate / at your earliest convenience

_____

_____

6.   any further information / please do not hesitate / if you need / to contact me

_____

_____

7.   an alternate suggestion / if / we would be pleased / you have / to consider it

_____

_____

8.   the results / we will send you / as soon as possible / of the competition

_____

_____

9.   to you / of some assistance / this information / i trust / will be

_____

_____

10. this explanation / i hope / will answer / you raised / the questions

_____

_____

Plugging Expressions into Letters   Exercise 4.7

Would these expressions be likely to occur in a beginning (B) or a closing (C) sentence or could they be used in both (BC)? Check the appropriate box.

		B	C	BC
1.	feel free to contact	☐	☐	☐
2.	please don't hesitate	☐	☐	☐
3.	in response to	☐	☐	☐
4.	once again	☐	☐	☐
5.	get in touch	☐	☐	☐
6.	at your earliest convenience	☐	☐	☐
7.	effective May 1	☐	☐	☐
8.	would assist me	☐	☐	☐
9.	may be able to help you	☐	☐	☐

		B	C	BC
10.	This is to inform you	☐	☐	☐
11.	I trust	☐	☐	☐
12.	as you may recall	☐	☐	☐
13.	as soon as possible	☐	☐	☐
14.	in accordance with	☐	☐	☐
15.	further to	☐	☐	☐
16.	Thank you for	☐	☐	☐
17.	would be appreciated	☐	☐	☐
18.	I enclose	☐	☐	☐

Communicating Arrangements   Exercise 4.8

You have made arrangements for a European-based consultant to visit your department for a three-week period. Write to him or her explaining the arrangements you have made for travel, accommodation, and reimbursement of expenses. Include details of ground transportation from the nearest airport.

Revise your draft carefully before you show it to the teacher.

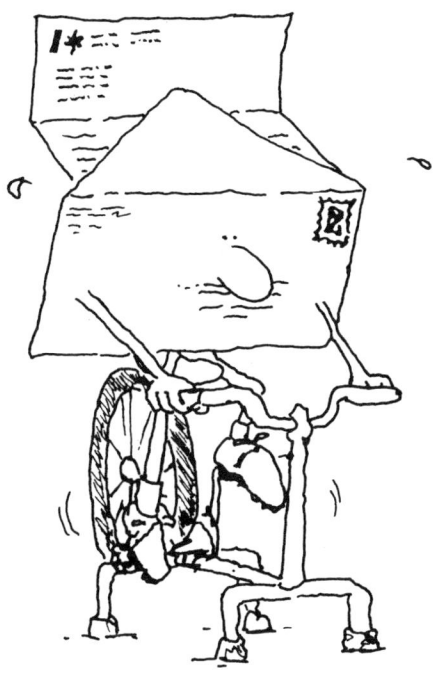

Unit 5   **Practising Letters**

Organizing and Punctuating   **Exercise 5.1**

The following letter was written as one long paragraph with inadequate punctuation. Rewrite the
letter with appropriate punctuation and paragraphing.

 Government   Gouvernement
of Canada   du Canada

Your file   Votre référence

Our file   Notre référence
5.1

February 29, 1988

Robert W. Dolbin
7 Ealey Cres.
Kentville, N.S.
B4N 4H1

Dear Sir,

Your letter of February 15 addressed to Information Canada
has been referred to this office. The information you are
seeking is the concern of several government departments,
in particular the Departments of Finance and of Energy
Mines and Resources as well as the Privy Council Office.
We are therefore sending a copy of your letter to each of
these departments. In the meantime the enclosed copy of
Our System of Government published by the Department of the
Secretary of State may be of some assistance to you.

Sincerely,

V.N. Radice
Information Officer

Canada

Organizing and Punctuating

The following letter was written as one long paragraph with inadequate punctuation. Rewrite the letter in four paragraphs, punctuating where necessary.

 Government   Gouvernement
of Canada   du Canada

Your file   Votre référence

Our file   Notre référence
5.2

December 18, 1989

Morag Fraser
248B Valiquette Avenue
Loretteville, Qc   G2B 1M4

Dear Ms. Fraser:

This will acknowledge receipt of your recent letter requesting information on immunization procedures preparatory to your trip to Burkina Faso. You are required to be in possession of a valid International Certificate of Vaccination against Yellow Fever. In addition, this department recommends that all travelers to this region be protected against polio tetanus and hepatitis A the vaccination booklet is available from your doctor. Please note that the record must include the name of the person vaccinated the date of vaccination the doctor's signature with an indication of his or her professional status and the origin and batch number of the vaccine used. Following this the booklet must be submitted to a Municipal Provincial or Federal health authority for application of the official validating stamp. We trust this is the information you require.

Sincerely,

J.W. Leighton
Chief
Information
Resources Section

Canada

Editing and Improving   **Exercise 5.3**

Using the suggestions given, rewrite this letter.
1. Paragraph 1 is a sentence fragment and is incorrectly punctuated.
2. The tone of this letter is too passive and impersonal; make it more dynamic and personal.

■✦ Government   Gouvernement
of Canada   du Canada

                                        Your file   Votre référence

                                        Our file   Notre référence
                                        5.3

Julia Morros
Recambios Automoviles
Calle Pablo Iglesias 53
28079 Madrid
Spain

                                        November 11, 1987

Dear Ms. Morros:

        In reply to your letter of October 31 1987
regarding automobile parts manufacturers interested in
exporting to Spain.

        It would be appreciated if we could be advised
regarding the type of automobile parts your client is
interested in. It would also be useful to us if we
knew whether original equipment parts or parts for the
service market are required by your client.

        When this information has been received by us,
we will be in a better position to advise you of
companies looking for export opportunities in Spain.

                        Sincerely yours,

                        Anne O'Shaughnessy
                        Export Programs Division

WD/la

Canadä

Editing and Improving

Using the suggestions given, rewrite this letter.

1. There is a sentence fragment in paragraph 1.
2. Paragraphs 2, 3, and 4 are too chatty for written correspondence and should not be separated. Combine paragraphs 2 and 3, and make the tone more neutral.
3. The closing is incorrect.

 Government   Gouvernement
of Canada   du Canada

Your file   Votre reference

Our file   Notre reference

5.4

1987-08-23

M. Fostad
P.O. Box 1341
Thompson, Manitoba
R8N 0L9

Dear M. Fostad:

Your recent letter to Indian and Northern Affairs Canada.
This correspondence has been referred to this office for
further action.

From your letter we cannot tell what kind of farmer you are
or what you want to grow. Enclosed are a couple of
publications dealing with Canadian farming and our list of
publications.

We are anxious to help you, M. Fostad. But, you know,
we've got to have more details about the type of farming
you're in and what your problems are.

We're waiting to hear from you.

Sincerely Yours.

Crop Development Division

Writing Role-Play   **Exercise 5.5**

1. The cafeteria in your office building is run by Bill's Catering Ltd. Food quality and service have deteriorated rapidly since the arrival of a new cafeteria manager.

> **OFFICE EMPLOYEE**
> As the senior staff person in your office, you have volunteered to write to the new cafeteria manager to complain. Be polite but firm, and outline specific problems with the service. Suggest several changes.

> **CAFETERIA MANAGER**
> You are aware of the dissatisfaction. But you were sent in to manage this cafeteria because you have been successful at cutting costs and raising profits. The manager before you was dismissed because of a steady decline in profits. Write a response in which you apologize for certain cutbacks in service and explain some of the reasons. Inform the office employee which of the suggested changes you are forced to reject.

2. D. Edwards, a staff trainer with Provincial Telephone Services, is looking for information to assist her or him in designing a managers' training course in conducting effective meetings. Edwards writes to the Public Service Commission's Staff Development Branch for assistance in designing the course.

> **EDWARDS**
> Write to M. Gagnon, a PSC training specialist, for information on objectives, content, and scheduling in similar courses for government employees. Ask for general information, but also request copies of any course outlines he or she might have.

> **GAGNON**
> Write a letter to D. Edwards in which you provide general information. Use the information in the course description. Decide how you will respond to the request for copies of course outlines.

A REMINDER

1. Check carefully to make sure you are using the correct title.
2. Indicate your subject and your purpose clearly in the first paragraph.
3. Convey your information in a clear and varied style.
4. Adjust your tone to suit the purpose, situation, and reader.

COURSE DESCRIPTION

2.18 T906 Conducting Effective Meetings*

2.18.1 Duration: 2 days

2.18.2 This course is for:

- those whose job functions regularly include conducting and attending meetings
- those who experience difficulty getting meetings underway, on time, and rolling
- those whose meetings often seem to fall far short of accomplishing concrete results.

2.18.3 At the end of this course, you will be able to:

- clearly define the roles and responsibilities of the chairperson and participants
- plan and organize your meetings around the decision to be made
- use techniques for starting your meetings and keeping them on time and on target
- deal with difficult problems posed by participants
- make meetings more productive.

2.18.4 Course Outline

1. Proper Focus for Meetings

   - the purpose of meetings: information, decisions, problem solving
   - problems with meetings — the views of participants
   - reasons for unproductive meetings
   - definitions of "meeting"

2. Pre-Meeting Considerations

   - determining the need for a meeting
   - alternatives
   - proper planning — the key to success of all activities
   - clarifying purpose and objectives
   - crisp, clear, accomplishable agenda
   - critical people only
   - physical setting
   - anticipating problems.

3. Considerations During Meeting

   - the role of the chairperson
   - process vs. content
   - using questions to control the meeting and to involve all members
   - problem people
   - roles of participants at meetings
     - doing your part before, during and after
     - responsibility for contributing
     - rotation of leadership role
   - taking minutes, formats

4. Post-Meeting Considerations

   - minutes
   - follow-up
   - progress reports
   - evaluating your meetings
     - what went wrong
     - how to make them better

5. Practice Meetings

   - each participant prepares an agenda and acts as chairperson for a 10-15 minute small group practice meeting
   - the meetings are video-taped, played back, and commented on by chairpersons and other participants
   - the trainer provides feedback, coaching and suggestions for improvement

* Source: *Personnel Management Manual, Volume 27: Courses and Educational Services of the Public Service Commission.* Ottawa: Public Service Commission of Canada. Reproduced with permission of the Minister of Supply and Services Canada.

PART THREE

AN APPLICATION

In this part you will prepare a curriculum vitae and a covering letter.

While the C.V. is important, the covering letter is your first chance to make an impression on a potential employer.

Unit 1   The Curriculum Vitae

The curriculum vitae (C.V.) or resumé is your biography in capsule form. It is a short record of your work experience, your education, your special expertise, and your personal interests. Very often it is the only document an employer will use to decide whether you meet basic qualifications for a position and should be interviewed.

PERSONAL INFORMATION

In addition to your name, address, and phone number(s), your C.V. should state your citizenship, Social Insurance Number, and language fluency.

WORK EXPERIENCE

Begin with your most recent position and list earlier positions in reverse chronological order. For each position, give the title of the job you held, the name and address of the employer, and, in point form, a short description of your responsibilities.

EDUCATION

Like work experience, education is often described in reverse chronological order. After citing the dates, name the degree or certificate you received or are working toward. Add "(incomplete)" if you did not complete a program. Also indicate the school or university and the name of the program.

OTHER SECTIONS

Depending on your experience and interests, you may wish to add other sections. For example, if you have given workshops for different audiences, you might make a Training Sessions category. If you have written articles for various periodicals, you will have a Publications section. If you have done volunteer work, it should be mentioned.

REFERENCES

Common practice is to state "References available upon request". Letters of recommendation may be attached to your C.V.

Writing your C.V.   **Exercise 1.1**

Look through the competition posters in your office or the Help Wanted section of a newspaper. Find a position that you might like to apply for. Prepare a curriculum vitae in response to the advertisement.

SAMPLE CURRICULUM VITAE

Elizabeth Smiley

Home: 170 Hillcrest Ave.
Ottawa, Ontario
K1B 7S7
(613) 874-3425

Office: Special Studies Team
180 Peter Street, Room 317
Ottawa, Ontario
K1R 7S7
(613) 923-7761

Languages: English fluent
Dene - knowledgeable
Some French

Social Insurance: 610-427-567

Career Experience:

Special Studies	1980 - present	Department of Indian and Northern Affairs Special research into life styles of native peoples; reporting on above; liaison with appropriate provincial departments
Research Assistant	1977 - 1980	Secretary of State Researching specific topics for inter-governmental discussions
Teaching Assistant	1972 - 1974	University of Alberta Assistant to Professor Peter Broadfoot for "Origins and Cultures of Native Peoples of the Tundra"

Other Experience:

Editor	1976 - 1979	The National Journal for Native Peoples
Case Worker	1972 (Summer)	Native Peoples Institute (Calgary) Volunteer worker to assist native people in adjusting to urban communities
Observer	1971 (Summer)	Associacion de los Indijenos (Chile) Official University of Alberta observer of governmental programs for integration of Chilean Indian tribes into urban settings

Education:

M.A. (Sociology)	1970 - 1972	University of Alberta (Edmonton) Thesis: The Contribution of Ethnic Minority Groups to the Canadian Mosaic
B.A. (Sociology)	1967 - 1970	Simon Fraser University (Burnaby, British Columbia)

References available on request

SAMPLE CURRICULUM VITAE

ELIZABETH J. SMILEY
170 Hillcrest Ave.
Ottawa, Ont. K1B 7S7
(613) 874-3425 (home)
(613) 923-7761 (office)

PERSONAL INFORMATION

DATE OF BIRTH: November 12, 1950

PLACE OF BIRTH: Brandon, Manitoba

CITIZENSHIP: Canadian

LANGUAGE FLUENCY: English - completely fluent
                    Dene - knowledgeable
                    Some French

MINIMUM SALARY: $37,500

DATE AVAILABLE: Within 30 days

EDUCATION

1970 - 1972   M.A. (Sociology), University of Alberta, Edmonton, Alberta
                Thesis: The Contribution of Ethnic Minority Groups to the Canadian Mosaic
1967 - 1970   B.A. (Sociology), Simon Fraser University, Burnaby, British Columbia

WORK EXPERIENCE

1980 to present   Special Studies Officer (Department of Indian and Northern Affairs,
                    Ottawa, Ontario)

                    Duties: conducting special investigations into various aspects of the lives
                             of native peoples;

                             writing reports on these investigations, including recommendations
                             where warranted; and

                             liaison with provincial governments and attending federal-
                             provincial conferences and meetings.

1974 - 1980   Research Assistant
                (Department of the Secretary of State, Ottawa, Ontario)

1972 - 1974   Teaching Assistant
                (University of Alberta, Edmonton, Ontario)

SPECIAL INTEREST

1976 - 1979   Editor, The National Journal for Native Peoples (Ottawa)

REFERENCES

1. Mr. George Watson, Director, Special Studies
    180 Peter Street, Ottawa, Ontario   K1R 7S7
    Phone: (613) 995-3923

2. Roberta Cornell, Head, Special Studies Team
    180 Peter Street, Ottawa, Ontario   K1R 7S7
    Phone: (613) 995-3927

3. Professor Peter Broadfoot, Chairman, Department of Sociology
    University of Alberta, Edmonton, Alberta T6G 2E1
    Phone: (403) 771-8723

Unit 2   The Covering Letter

The covering letter which accompanies the C.V. is your first chance to make an impression on a potential employer. If the covering letter is weak, even a good C.V. may not be read.

THE BEGINNING

The way you begin a covering letter depends largely on the circumstances. Here are some common job application situations and some suggestions for beginnings.

Response to a Poster, Circular, or Newspaper Advertisement.

If you are applying for a position advertised in a newspaper or elsewhere, you will probably want to mention this in your first sentence.

> **In response to your advertisement in the *Journal* of Saturday, June 24, I wish to submit my application for the position of Director of Public Relations.**

> **I would like to be considered for the position of Removal Insurance Officer advertised in to-day's *Journal*.**

> **I am writing in response to your recent advertisement in the *Journal*, which invited applications for the position of Affirmative Action Co-ordinator.**

Following Up a Suggestion

If you have heard about an opening through someone you know, you may want to mention her or his name. In the following beginnings, the assumption is that the writer feels that it is advantageous to mention the source of information and that the people quoted have agreed to the use of their names.

> **I am writing to you at the suggestion of Lawrence Madsen, who indicated that you might be interested in someone with my background and qualifications.**

> **Dr. Anita Young suggested that I write to you in connection with an opening for a communications systems engineer in your department.**

> **I would like to apply for the position of Reference Archivist which Mr. L. Tumanoff tells me is currently being staffed.**

If you do not want to acknowledge the source of your information, you can begin by writing:

> **I understand that you may have an opening for a marine biologist.**

> **I have been given to understand that you are currently recruiting for a vacancy in the Policy Analyst category.**

> **I wish to be considered for the position of Emergency Planning Officer that I understand is currently being staffed.**

General Enquiry about the Availability of Jobs

If you don't know whether there are any vacancies, you might begin a letter of enquiry:

> **I am writing to enquire about job opportunities for junior geologists.**

> **I am writing in the hope that you may have openings for consulting statisticians.**

> **I would like to be considered for a position as a records clerk in your department.**

THE BODY

In the body of your covering letter, mention one or two advantages, from the employer's point of view, of hiring you. Be sure to avoid bragging or being pushy and to maintain a polite, neutral-to-formal tone.

THE FINAL PARAGRAPH

The final paragraph should offer to provide any other information or details the prospective employer might want.

SAMPLE COVERING LETTER

```
                                    10 Hillcrest Avenue
                                    Ottawa, Ontario
                                    K1B 7S7


T. Towe, Personnel Advisor
Indian and Northern Affairs Canada
Alberta Place, Suite 1010
Calgary, Alberta
T6S 2C1


                                    August 26, 1987

Dear Mr. Towe:

     I am writing in response to an interdepartmental
circular advertising a Senior Project Officer position
in your region (No. 87-INA-CAL-CCID-152).  I am very
interested in such a position.

     For the past five years, I have been employed as a
Special Studies Officer with the Department of Indian
and Northern Affairs in Ottawa and have been working on
a variety of projects in connection with Native organi-
zations.  My work has been both challenging and stimu-
lating; however, I feel that I would now like to move
into a position of greater responsibility.

     I am enclosing a copy of my curriculum vitae and
will gladly provide any further information you may
require.

                                    Yours truly,

                                    Elizabeth J. Smiley

                                    Elizabeth J. Smiley
```

Writing a Covering Letter

Exercise 2.1

Write a covering letter that you would attach to the C.V. you wrote in Unit 1.

PART FOUR

STUDYING
MEMOS & LETTERS

In this part you will find a selection of sample memos and letters. Study questions are provided to help you focus on specific points.

Exercise 1

Government   Gouvernement
of Canada   du Canada   **MEMORANDUM   NOTE DE SERVICE**

SECURITY · CLASSIFICATION · DE SÉCURITÉ	

TO Ralph Lester
À   Licence Control

OUR FILE – N / RÉFÉRENCE

1

YOUR FILE – V / RÉFÉRENCE

FROM K.C. Sawyer, Director
DE   Resource Development Service

DATE
30 January 1986

SUBJECT
OBJET   Oyster Leases

In reply to your memo of January 16, I attach two application
forms (F-620) for oyster leases for Mrs. Florence McLaurin and
Herman A. MacKinnon. Please see that the applicants receive
the forms.

After completion by each applicant, the forms should be returned
to you. The applications will be recorded, and, when our field
officers have an opportunity, they will examine the areas applied
for. If conditions are satisfactory, the boundaries of each area
will be surveyed and leases will be sent for signature.

K.C. Sawyer
K.C. Sawyer

Attach. (2)

1. a) Which of the strategies on the right are used in this memo?*
    b) What expressions are used to signal the strategies?

2. Is the general tone of the memo polite and neutral or personal
    and direct?

3. Does the memo require a closing sentence? If so, suggest an
    appropriate one.

Acknowledging
Apologizing
Buying Time
Complaining
Congratulating
Conveying Bad News
Conveying Good News
Criticizing
Expecting
Expressing Goodwill
Informing
Predicting
Recalling
Refusing/Rejecting
Regretting
Requesting
Suggesting
Thanking
Urging

---

* The list is not intended to be complete. Other strategies may also be found in
these exercises.

Exercise 2

| Government Gouvernement of Canada du Canada | **MEMORANDUM** | **NOTE DE SERVICE** |

		SECURITY · CLASSIFICATION · DE SÉCURITÉ
TO **A**	Brenda Chalmers Research Officer	OUR FILE – N / RÉFÉRENCE 2
FROM **DE**	T.H. Tomlinson Director Information Services	YOUR FILE – V / RÉFÉRENCE
		DATE 31 January 1985

SUBJECT OBJET   CONSERVATION INFORMATION

      In answer to your memo of January 25, we have pleasure in sending you information on conservation of fish, plus a copy of the Annual Report of the Fisheries Research Board of Canada. We have also contacted the Canadian Wildlife Service here in Ottawa, who will shortly be sending you their data on conservation of fish.

      We hope this information will be useful to you.

T.H. Tomlinson

T.H. Tomlinson

TT/AG

Att: 2

Acknowledging
Apologizing
Buying Time
Complaining
Congratulating
Conveying Bad News
Conveying Good News
Criticizing
Expecting
Expressing Goodwill
Informing
Predicting
Recalling
Refusing/Rejecting
Regretting
Requesting
Suggesting
Thanking
Urging

1. a) Which of the strategies on the right are used in this memo?
    b) What expressions are used to signal the strategies?

2. Is the general tone of the memo polite and neutral or personal and direct?

3. The memo is brief. Is there any other information that might be necessary?

4. Is the closing sentence appropriate? Suggest another closing that maintains the same tone.

■✦ Government   Gouvernement
of Canada   du Canada

MEMORANDUM   NOTE DE SERVICE

TO
A   N.J. Conklin
Chief Oceanographer
Marine Sciences Branch

FROM
DE   W.M. Wolfe
Director
Fisheries Services

SECURITY · CLASSIFICATION · DE SÉCURITÉ

OUR FILE – N / RÉFÉRENCE
3

YOUR FILE – V / RÉFÉRENCE

DATE
February 1, 1987

SUBJECT
OBJET   Sneed Application

Further to our telephone conversation this afternoon, you will
find attached copies of a letter from J. Sneed and enclosures.
It is my understanding that you will forward this material to
the appropriate office.

W. M. Wolfe
W.M. Wolfe

Attachments: 3

1. a) Which of the strategies on the right are used in this memo?
    b) What expressions are used to signal the strategies?

2. Does the length of the memo seem appropriate?

3. What is the purpose of the expression "It is my under-
    standing that ..."? What was the agreement made in the
    telephone conversation?

4. Does a closing sentence seem necessary?

Acknowledging
Apologizing
Buying Time
Complaining
Congratulating
Conveying Bad News
Conveying Good News
Criticizing
Expecting
Expressing Goodwill
Informing
Predicting
Recalling
Refusing/Rejecting
Regretting
Requesting
Suggesting
Thanking
Urging

Exercise 4

| ■✦ Government Gouvernement | **MEMORANDUM** | **NOTE DE SERVICE** |
| of Canada du Canada | | |

TO À	Brenda MacKenzie Consumer Consultant	SECURITY · CLASSIFICATION · DE SÉCURITÉ
		OUR FILE – N / RÉFÉRENCE 4
FROM DE	Mabel Fries Chief Consumer Branch	YOUR FILE – V / RÉFÉRENCE
		DATE March 19, 1986

SUBJECT
OBJET   <u>Salt and Sodium Content in Fish</u>

This is in answer to your query regarding salt and sodium content of fresh and frozen fish.

The Inspection Service, Department of Fisheries states:

"In general, fresh (unfrozen) fish and fish products do not contain added salt. On the other hand, frozen fish products may or may not have added salt depending on the methods used by the particular processor (i.e. fillet dips prior to packaging and freezing in order to reduce thaw drip). Where these dips are employed, the dip may contain either common salt or sodium tripolyphosphate."

Enclosed is a table of "Sodium Content of Fish Flesh" which was adapted from the <u>American Dietetic Journal</u>. Unfortunately I do not have the reference, but it appeared 5 or 6 years ago. This was for fresh products.

Do you have Handbook No. 8, U.S. Department of Agriculture? If not, please let us know, and we will order a copy for you. This handbook contains a good deal of information on fish. The Fisheries Research Board is preparing a publication containing Canadian figures, but it is not available yet.

In 1982 the Montreal Civic Hospital did an analysis on frozen haddock fillets and they reported as follows:

Sodium – 55.3 mg per 100 mg of wet fish
Chlorides as NaCL – 151.6 mg per 100 mg of wet fish.

M. Fries
M. Fries

---

1. a) Which of the strategies on the right are used in this memo?
   b) What expressions are used to signal the strategies?

2. How many sources of information does the writer provide? Does the memo seem comprehensive? What is the main purpose of the memo?

3. Is the general tone of the memo polite and informal or polite and neutral?

4. Could the memo be improved by adding a closing sentence? If so, suggest an appropriate one.

5. What gives the memo its tone?

Acknowledging
Apologizing
Buying Time
Complaining
Congratulating
Conveying Bad News
Conveying Good News
Criticizing
Expecting
Expressing Goodwill
Informing
Predicting
Recalling
Refusing/Rejecting
Regretting
Requesting
Suggesting
Thanking
Urging

Exercise 5

■◆ Government Gouvernement
of Canada du Canada

MEMORANDUM   **NOTE DE SERVICE**

TO / A ▶	D.M. Preville Director
FROM / DE	J. Cosgrove Chief Aids to Navigation

SECURITY · CLASSIFICATION · DE SÉCURITÉ

OUR FILE – N / RÉFÉRENCE
5

YOUR FILE – V / RÉFÉRENCE

DATE 1985-05-19

SUBJECT / OBJET   **Repair Claim**

> I refer to your memo of May 5 with an attachment concerning the claim for repairs to a boat which reportedly struck one of the department's winter markers.

> CCGS "Phoenix" placed lighted buoy 75T on April 28; however, the buoy report card covering the installation has not yet been received in the office. "Phoenix" is presently in Lake Erie and a message received from the Master in reply to our query indicates that the vessel was unable to find the winter marker and believed it to be carried away by ice.

> CCGS "Saxon" again checked the area on May 11 around buoy 57T and finally located the winter marker 100 feet east and south of the proper buoy position with approximately 6 inches of water over the spar. It is quite possible that the vessel in question did strike this marker. However, it is a fact that the winter marker was dragged off station into slightly deeper water and was submerged.

> Please advise if further action is required by this office.

J. Cosgrove
J. Cosgrove

---

1. a) Which of the strategies on the right are used in this memo?
    b) What expressions are used to signal the strategies?
2. What happened to the unnamed boat referred to by the writer?
3. Where was the winter marker?
4. Was the winter marker responsible for the damage to the unnamed boat? What is the main purpose of the memo?
5. Is the general tone of the memo polite and neutral or personal and informal?

Acknowledging **Apologizing** **Buying Time** **Complaining** **Congratulating** **Conveying Bad News** **Conveying Good News** **Criticizing** **Expecting** **Expressing Goodwill** **Informing** **Predicting** **Recalling** **Refusing/Rejecting** **Regretting** **Requesting** **Suggesting** **Thanking** **Urging**

NOTES

Buoy: a floating object anchored in a certain place to warn or guide ships

Winter marker: a special buoy placed in the ice during the winter to mark the location of a summer buoy which is removed in the winter

CCGS: The abbreviation for Canadian Coast Guard Ship

Exercise 6

◼✦ Government   Gouvernement
of Canada   du Canada

MEMORANDUM   NOTE DE SERVICE

TO ▸ B. Miller	SECURITY · CLASSIFICATION · DE SÉCURITÉ
À Liaison Officer	
	OUR FILE – N / RÉFÉRENCE
	6
FROM C. Romonoski	YOUR FILE – V / RÉFÉRENCE
DE Director, Policy and Research	
	DATE
	30 December 1988

SUBJECT
OBJET   <u>Services Available to Provincial Governments</u>

In a memorandum dated December 16, 1988, you asked for
information concerning the services available to provincial
governments from federal agencies.

As far as the Transportation Policy and Research Branch is
concerned, I think one could say that we provide economic
and operational advice on transportation by air, by sea, by
rail and by road. On occasion, I would imagine that our
services could be made available to provincial governments
on a consultative basis, but we are not staffed to perform
such a function in any extensive way.

We could, however, participate in an exchange of information
since provincial governments often have their own economic
and policy staff to provide advice in those areas falling
within provincial responsibilities.

Catherine Romonoski

C. Romonoski

CR/GM

Acknowledging
Apologizing
Buying Time
Complaining
Congratulating
Conveying Bad News
Conveying Good News
Criticizing
Expecting
Expressing Goodwill
Informing
Predicting
Recalling
Refusing/Rejecting
Regretting
Requesting
Suggesting
Thanking
Urging

1. a) Which of the strategies on the right are used in this memo?
   b) What expressions are used to signal the strategies?

2. What information does the branch provide for provincial
   governments?

3. Is the general tone of the memo formal and cautious or
   personal?

4. What language choices set the tone of the memo?

Exercise 7

Government   Gouvernement
of Canada   du Canada   **MEMORANDUM   NOTE DE SERVICE**

	SECURITY · CLASSIFICATION · DE SÉCURITÉ

TO
À ▶ J. Strong
Director

OUR FILE – N / RÉFÉRENCE

7

YOUR FILE – V / RÉFÉRENCE

FROM
DE   H. Reese
Field Officer

DATE
October 10, 1987

SUBJECT
OBJET   **A.N.O. Series V, No. 10, Wickaninnish Beach Park**
(Long Island) Vancouver Island, B.C.

This refers to your memo of October 2, 1987, requesting supporting
detail in regard to the closure of the park to aircraft traffic.

I am attaching copies of correspondence between the Department and
the Provincial Department of Recreation and Conservation, Victoria,
and between the Department and the R.C.M.P. The correspondence, I
believe, is self-explanatory.

Briefly, the Long Beach portion of the park has been used as a
landing strip by light aircraft for many years. Originally this
posed no problem, as road access to the area was limited to the
use of logging roads from Port Alberni, thus restricting the amount
of traffic. This has now given way to a good provincial highway
and opened up a veritable paradise for family campers who pitch
their tents along the edge of the beach and occupy the sand area
used by the aircraft.

This developed through the years into what we considered a hazardous
situation. Further, I wish to point out that Tofino Airport is
directly adjacent to a portion of the beach and within walking
distance from one corner of the airport.

Also enclosed for your files are copies of the pertinent Orders in
Council relating to the formation of the park.

H Reese

H. Reese

Encl. 2

Acknowledging
Apologizing
Buying Time
Complaining
Congratulating
Conveying Bad News
Conveying Good News
Criticizing
Expecting
Expressing Goodwill
Informing
Predicting
Recalling
Refusing/Rejecting
Regretting
Requesting
Suggesting
Thanking
Urging

1. a) Which of the strategies on the right are used in this memo?
    b) What expressions are used to signal the strategies?

2. Why was Long Beach closed to air traffic?

3. Would a more informal tone be appropriate?

4. Could the memo be improved by the addition of a closing
    sentence? If so, suggest one.

Exercise 8

▮✦ Government Gouvernement of Canada du Canada	**MEMORANDUM**	**NOTE DE SERVICE**

TO A ➤ A.M. Loken	SECURITY · CLASSIFICATION · DE SÉCURITÉ
	OUR FILE – N / RÉFÉRENCE 8
FROM DE H. Hopkins	YOUR FILE – V / RÉFÉRENCE
	DATE 8 September 1986

SUBJECT OBJET   EASEMENT AGREEMENT

I am enclosing the agreement forms, which were passed along to us by Roger Brown in your absence, to cover a Communication Corporation Easement over part of the property owned by Hansen's Feed Lot in the Township of Fertile Valley.

We have found the documents to be in order, except that provision should be made to maintain the present access road to the hydro substation. The survey map shows that the proposed easement will cross the access road to the hydro substation at approximately Intersection B.

The document should be implemented in order to become effective prior to August 1, 1987.

We would appreciate your arranging formal implementation with Hansen's Feed Lot.

H. Hopkins
H. Hopkins

Enc. 3.

---

1. a) Which of the strategies on the right are used in this memo?
   b) What expressions are used to signal the strategies?

2. Is the subject line clearly related to the contents of the memo?

3. Is the tone critical and formal or neutral and polite?

Acknowledging
Apologizing
Buying Time
Complaining
Congratulating
Conveying Bad News
Conveying Good News
Criticizing
Expecting
Expressing Goodwill
Informing
Predicting
Recalling
Refusing/Rejecting
Regretting
Requesting
Suggesting
Thanking
Urging

NOTE

Easement: a legal right held by one person or agent on land owned by another. For example, a utility company can claim a legal right to clear wooded land on private property in order to erect transmission towers.

Exercise 9

■✦ Government Gouvernement of Canada du Canada	**MEMORANDUM NOTE DE SERVICE**

TO
À ▶ R.J. Kincaid
Project Analyst

FROM
DE D.J. Butler
Assistant Director General

SECURITY · CLASSIFICATION · DE SÉCURITÉ

OUR FILE – N / RÉFÉRENCE
9

YOUR FILE – V / RÉFÉRENCE

DATE
4 February 1988

SUBJECT
OBJET   Finance Study Information

Your January 27 memo asked me for my view on the federal government's most pressing problem, and I should not wish to reply in
a cryptic or abbreviated way.

I enclose a copy of the June 3, 1987, budget speech and related
papers. I have announced through this office that the next speech
will be presented in early March; it will contain a fresh statement of the government's views on this whole matter.

I hope the study your department is overseeing is still open at
that time.

D.J. Butler
D.J. Butler

Enclosure

DJB/ry

Acknowledging **Apologizing** **Buying Time** **Complaining** **Congratulating** **Conveying Bad News** **Conveying Good News** **Criticizing** **Expecting** **Expressing Goodwill** **Informing** **Predicting** **Recalling** **Refusing/Rejecting** **Regretting** **Requesting** **Suggesting** **Thanking** **Urging**

1. a) Which of the strategies on the right are used in this memo?
   b) What expressions are used to signal the strategies?
2. What is implied in the first paragraph?
3. Is the general tone of the memo direct or cautious?
4. Would the closing paragraph be more appropriate if it
   included an expression of regret?

Exercise 10

▮✳ Government Gouvernement	**MEMORANDUM** **NOTE DE SERVICE**

TO
À ▶ K. Roberts

FROM
DE   R. Bhattacharya

SECURITY · CLASSIFICATION · DE SÉCURITÉ
OUR FILE – N / RÉFÉRENCE 10
YOUR FILE – V / RÉFÉRENCE
DATE June 7, 1985

SUBJECT
OBJET   Conference Preparations

I have recently received your department's useful list of topics for the upcoming conference, Industrial Development for the Eighties.

As well as the list of topics you have sent, would it be possible for you to provide me with a list of your members who would be interested in attending the conference? May I suggest that you use the attached form on which the names, addresses, and other relevant information can be listed.

I would also like to suggest that you provide me with a list of qualified people who, in your opinion, could make a significant contribution by presenting papers, or by participating as principal speakers or on discussion panels.

It is my intention to have our first mailing out within the next few weeks, and, for this reason, an early reply would be helpful.

R. Bhattacharya
R. Bhattacharya

Att: 1

RB/jp

---

1. a) Which of the strategies on the right are used in this memo?
    b) What expressions are used to signal the strategies?
2. Is there an indication that Roberts has sent insufficient information?
3. Is the general tone of the memo informal and aggressive or polite and neutral?
4. Would the tone of the memo be different if the closing paragraph began "I hope to ..."?

Strategies
Acknowledging
Apologizing
Buying Time
Complaining
Congratulating
Conveying Bad News
Conveying Good News
Criticizing
Expecting
Expressing Goodwill
Informing
Predicting
Recalling
Refusing/Rejecting
Regretting
Requesting
Suggesting
Thanking
Urging

Government   Gouvernement
of Canada   du Canada

Your file   Votre reference

Our file   Notre reference

11

June 3, 1985

Dr. M. Creeley
Ottawa Bureau, Medical Services
Health and Welfare Canada
708 Albert St.
Ottawa, Ont. K1H 7B9

Dear Dr. Creeley:

I am writing in reference to your letter of May 23
concerning our employee, C.W. Bryant.

We have been informed that Mr. Bryant has returned to
work, claims to be fit, and no longer wishes to submit
to a medical examination.

We must therefore request that you discontinue your
investigation of this case.

Yours truly,

R. Bancroft, Chief
Personnel Services, Air

RB/rb

Acknowledging
Apologizing
Buying Time
Complaining
Congratulating
Conveying Bad News
Conveying Good News
Criticizing
Expecting
Expressing Goodwill
Informing
Predicting
Recalling
Refusing/Rejecting
Regretting
Requesting
Suggesting
Thanking
Urging

1. a) Which of the strategies on the right are used in this letter?
    b) What expressions are used to signal the strategies?

2. What is the tone of this letter? Is it appropriate?

3. Should the letter have more detail?

4. Would a closing paragraph be appropriate?

Exercise 12

Government   Gouvernement
of Canada   du Canada

Your file   Votre reference

Our file   Notre reference
12

December 15, 1988

Mr. D.W. Thornton
Secretary
The Textiles Institute
230 Peel Street West
Montréal, P.Q.   H2K 3W3

Dear Mr. Thornton,

I am writing with regard to the overdue data on Canadian
fabrics shipments.

I would urge you to submit the above data to me no later
than January 25, 1989, in order that we can complete our
reports on schedule. Furthermore, it is essential that
you submit the data in the following sub-categories:
nylon fabrics, denim fabrics, and synthetic fabrics.

Thank you for your cooperation in this matter.

Yours truly,

A.A. Darnely, Director
International Economic Relations

/jp

Acknowledging
Apologizing
Buying Time
Complaining
Congratulating
Conveying Bad News
Conveying Good News
Criticizing
Expecting
Expressing Goodwill
Informing
Predicting
Recalling
Refusing/Rejecting
Regretting
Requesting
Suggesting
Thanking
Urging

1. a) Which of the strategies on the right are used in this letter?
   b) What expressions are used to signal the strategies?

2. What is the tone of the letter?

3. Would suggesting expressions be more appropriate?

4. Would a different closing sentence be more appropriate?
   Why? Why not?

Exercise 13

 **Government   Gouvernement
of Canada   du Canada**

Your file   Votre référence

Our file   Notre référence

13

February 10, 1989

Gail M. Craig
557 Mountain Rd.
Fort Collins
Colorado, U.S.A.

Dear Ms. Craig:

   Thank you for your letter of January 9 and your
interest in scientific vacancies with the Forestry Research
Board.

   I have forwarded copies of your letter and curriculum
vitae to directors of stations in Chibougamau, Quebec, and
Winnipeg, Manitoba. Those directors have the
responsibility for recruiting staff in research programs
that might be of interest to you.

   Unfortunately, at the present time I do not anticipate
any openings in the central research laboratories in
Ottawa, but perhaps the station directors will contact you
if suitable positions should become available.

   May I take this opportunity to wish you success in
finding suitable employment.

                    Yours sincerely,

                    TRKitsz

                    Theresa R. Kitsz
                    Personnel Officer

**Acknowledging
Apologizing
Buying Time
Complaining
Congratulating
Conveying Bad News
Conveying Good News
Criticizing
Expecting
Expressing Goodwill
Informing
Predicting
Recalling
Refusing/Rejecting
Regretting
Requesting
Suggesting
Thanking
Urging**

1. a) Which of the strategies on the right are used in this letter?
    b) What expressions are used to signal the strategies?

2. What is the first indication in the letter that the request is being
    refused?

3. What is the intent of the last paragraph?

Exercise 14

Government   Gouvernement
of Canada   du Canada

Your file   Votre reference

Our file   Notre reference

14

January 31, 1987

T. Norman
Regional Director
Canada Post
141 Murray St.
Charlottetown, P.E.I.
C1A 5T7

Dear T. Norman:

     I am writing in reference to your letter of January
25 concerning the proposed visit to our department of
Mr. K. Ingram.

     Because of a number of meetings and other
commitments involving the Director and the Assistant
Director during the week of February 27, it would not be
convenient for Mr. Ingram to come at that time.

     We would suggest instead that he arrange his visit
for the week of March 4. If this is suitable, would you
kindly let us know and we will arrange hotel accommodation.

Yours sincerely,

H. Bell

H. Bell, Director
Information and Consumer Services

/mp

Acknowledging
Apologizing
Buying Time
Complaining
Congratulating
Conveying Bad News
Conveying Good News
Criticizing
Expecting
Expressing Goodwill
Informing
Predicting
Recalling
Refusing/Rejecting
Regretting
Requesting
Suggesting
Thanking
Urging

1. a) Which of the strategies on the right are used in this letter?
     b) What expressions are used to signal the strategies?

2. Is the general tone of this letter formal and neutral or informal
and friendly?

3. In the last paragraph, why is the suggesting expression
appropriate?

Exercise 15

Government   Gouvernement
of Canada   du Canada

Your file   Votre reference

Our file   Notre reference

Dr. D. McLeod   15
Room 109
Science Building
University of Manitoba
Winnipeg, Manitoba   R2N 5S4

May 4, 1988

Dear Dr. McLeod:

Thank you for the opportunity to meet your graduating
class to discuss with them the training that they have
received. I sincerely hope that your students' assess-
ments of the interest and opportunities in my department's work were favourable and that some will present
themselves as candidates for present and future positions
in our Pollution Control Section.

My representatives, K.J. Jacks, R. Mbota, and W. Parker,
have asked me to forward their personal thanks for the
courtesies and assistance that you provided them.

If my department can be of any assistance to you in the
future, please do not hesitate to contact me.

Yours sincerely,

C. H. Marsh

C.H. Marsh, Director
Resource Development Service

/rg

Acknowledging
Apologizing
Buying Time
Complaining
Congratulating
Conveying Bad News
Conveying Good News
Criticizing
Expecting
Expressing Goodwill
Informing
Predicting
Recalling
Refusing/Rejecting
Regretting
Requesting
Suggesting
Thanking
Urging

1. a) Which of the strategies on the right are used in this letter?
    b) What expressions are used to signal the strategies?

2. C. Marsh thanks Dr. McLeod twice. Is this appropriate?

3. Is the tone of this letter personal or formal?

Exercise 16

 Government   Gouvernement
of Canada   du Canada

Your file   Votre référence

Our file   Notre référence

16

Patricia M. Soper   September 15, 1988
2992 Avenue Rd.
Toronto, Ont. M6Y 2T3

Dear Madam,

    Stephen Robertson has asked me to reply to your
letter concerning government policy on foreign control of
Canadian business activities.

    A number of considerations influence government
policy in this area. One is that direct foreign investment
has been very important to the development and expansion of
the Canadian economy. It has enabled us to exploit
resources which might have otherwise remained untouched for
many years; it has also assisted in the growth of the
manufacturing sector through the provision of risk capital,
technology and managerial skills.

    Thus, in general, direct foreign investment has
contributed to the standard of living which we now enjoy;
and, if we are to maintain and improve our living
standards, even larger investment will be required in the
future, both from Canadians and foreigners.

    For a historical perspective on the question,
Mr. Robertson has asked me to refer you to the following
sources, both of which are quite comprehensive:

1. Foreign-Owned Subsidiaries in Canada, a report by the
    Department of Trade and Commerce, 1984.

2. The Performance of Foreign-Owned Firms in Canada, a
    report by Professor A.E. Smith sponsored by the
    Canadian-American Committee and released in 1977.

    I hope this will be of some assistance to you.

              Yours very truly,

              T. Larsen

              T. Larsen
              Executive Assistant

Acknowledging
Apologizing
Buying Time
Complaining
Congratulating
Conveying Bad News
Conveying Good News
Criticizing
Expecting
Expressing Goodwill
Informing
Predicting
Recalling
Refusing/Rejecting
Regretting
Requesting
Suggesting
Thanking
Urging

1. a) Which of the strategies on the right are used in this letter?
    b) What expressions are used to signal the strategies?

2. This letter is in answer to a letter criticizing and questioning
    government policy. Is the tone appropriate?

3. Is the last sentence appropriate?

Exercise 17

  Government   Gouvernement
   of Canada   du Canada

Your file   Votre référence

Our file   Notre référence
17

March 1, 1988

D.A. Rose
Assistant General Manager
Eastern Marine Trust Company
4410 Waverly Road
St. John, New Brunswick   E2L 4V4

Dear Mr. Rose:

This is in reply to your letter of January 3 on the issue of payments to Inlet Packing Limited.

I must explain that we are somewhat at a loss to understand your request that monies owing, if any, to the owner of Inlet Packing Limited under the agreement of February 23, 1984, be paid to the Eastern Marine Trust Company. This department is in no way party to any arrangements between the trust company and its stockholders, and at no time was the department authorized by power of attorney to make payments to any other party of monies due under Clause 7, paragraph (e), sub-paragraph IV.

I should also point out that the $44,000.00 annual allotment is not in any way a subsidy but rather a payment for services rendered. Such a payment in any year is dependent on the rendering of services to the satisfaction of the Minister.

In the circumstances, I fail to see on what basis this department is obliged to subsidize stockholders in your company.

I can assure you this department is watching negotiations with a view to protecting the Minister's interests under the agreement referred to above.

Yours very truly,

W. T. Lawrence

W.T. Lawrence, Chief
Special Services Division
Regional Development Service

1. a) Which of the strategies on the right are used in this letter?
    b) What expressions are used to signal the strategies?

2. Do the expressions help to convey an angry and critical tone or a neutral and formal tone?

3. The trust company manager has clearly annoyed W. T. Lawrence.   What appears to be a likely cause of the annoyance?

4. Is the tone of the letter appropriate?

Acknowledging
Apologizing
Buying Time
Complaining
Congratulating
Conveying Bad News
Conveying Good News
Criticizing
Expecting
Expressing Goodwill
Informing
Predicting
Recalling
Refusing/Rejecting
Regretting
Requesting
Suggesting
Thanking
Urging

Exercise 18

 Government   Gouvernement
of Canada   du Canada

Your file   Votre référence

Our file   Notre référence

W. Collins   18
39 Blackheath Drive
Nepean, Ontario
K2E 5R9

3 August 1987

Dear Ms. Collins:

Re: Second Level Reply, Grievance No. 87-Y-OH-43(9)

I have carefully reviewed the facts of your grievance and the requested corrective actions. A hearing was held on the 31 of July 1987 at which your union representative was present.

As for your first and fourth corrective actions, I must inform you that personnel management planning and appointment to a given position is a managerial responsibility based on the need of human resources in a given context. The decision not to fill indeterminate positions was based on the certainty of a declining clientele. If and when the employer decides to appoint from the list, you may rest assured that the applicable act and regulations will be respected.

Your second and third corrective actions are granted to the extent of the letter of understanding between management and your union local signed on the 24 of June 1987. As for your fifth corrective action, since your grievance was presented at first level by your union representative and since an appropriate answer can be given at this level, a decision to do so was taken.

Yours truly,

C. Fehr

C. Fehr
Director

Acknowledging
Apologizing
Buying Time
Complaining
Congratulating
Conveying Bad News
Conveying Good News
Criticizing
Expecting
Expressing Goodwill
Informing
Predicting
Recalling
Refusing/Rejecting
Regretting
Requesting
Suggesting
Thanking
Urging

1. a) Which of the strategies on the right are used in this letter?
    b) What expressions are used to signal the strategies?

2. What is being rejected in this letter?

3. What effect does the final paragraph have on the tone of the letter?

4. Could the letter be improved by adding a closing expression?

Exercise 19

 Government   Gouvernement
of Canada   du Canada

May 14, 1988

Mr. R.M. Brookes
198 Simpson St.
Yellowknife, N.W.T.   X1A 2W9

Your file   votre reference

Our file   Notre reference

19

Dear Mr. Brookes:

I have now completed a detailed investigation into the matter of your
unanswered correspondence. I quite agree with you that this is a most
undesirable situation which should never have occurred. It is obvious
that no excuse can be made for not replying to your legitimate
request. However, I would like to try to explain what did transpire.

First, there is the matter of your letters of May 1985 to the Toronto
Regional Office. Although these letters are on file, there is no
record that a reply was ever forwarded. Since the employees concerned
are no longer employed in the Personnel Office, I could not determine
why this omission occurred.

Your letter of June 9, 1986, to our Ottawa office was referred to me
and replied to on July 16, 1986. A copy of this letter was forwarded
to the Toronto office with a request that they ensure that you were
paid any retroactive remuneration to which you were entitled. From my
letter you apparently assumed that I was the Personnel Director at
Toronto, and subsequently forwarded further correspondence to me at the
old Toronto office address. For that reason, and because you used the
wrong address, I did not receive your letters. However, the fact
remains that they were received in Toronto, and they should have
replied to you. In this regard, I can only assure you that corrective
action has been taken.

The matter of your retroactive salary has also been reviewed. Based on
our calculations you are entitled to approximately $490.00 and action
has been taken to effect payment immediately. It is expected that a
cheque will be issued by Central Pay Office in approximately 4 to 6
weeks and will be forwarded to you from this office. I regret that
what should have been a simple matter has become so involved and has
caused you such difficulty.

Once again, may I offer you my sincere apologies for the problems and
anxiety created by this situation.

Yours truly,

M.S Newton

Mary S. Newton
Chief, Personnel Services

Acknowledging
Apologizing
Buying Time
Complaining
Congratulating
Conveying Bad News
Conveying Good News
Criticizing
Expecting
Expressing Goodwill
Informing
Predicting
Recalling
Refusing/Rejecting
Regretting
Requesting
Suggesting
Thanking
Urging

1. a) Which of the strategies on the right are used in this letter?
    b) What expressions are used to signal the strategies?

2. Why is there so much information in the letter?

3. What is the tone of the letter?

4. Is the final apology effective?

Exercise 20

 Government Gouvernement
of Canada du Canada

Your file Votre référence

Our file Notre référence
20

October 29, 1986

Mr. J.R. Britnell, Director
Public Works Canada
444 - 26th Avenue
Shawinigan, Qué. G9N 1B5

Dear Mr. Britnell:

Further to my letter to you on October 1, I
enclose a copy of a letter dated August 2, 1986, from Mr.
C. Lang, Chief, Building Management.

I am not satisfied with Mr. Lang's response
because he does not answer the points I raised in my
letter. He suggests that a current policy should not be
made retroactive. It should be clear that this department
is not attempting to make a current decision retroactive;
we are merely asking for a facility which was agreed upon
in the original contract and promised to our employees on
that basis.

Your department contracted for the tapping-on of
the fresh air vents and for the designing and construction
of the lounge areas throughout the building.

The continued delay in equipping these lounge
areas and re-discussion of the original contract serve no
useful purpose. Moreover, the lack of action does nothing
to alleviate the serious employee discontent in the
building.

In view of the above, I would appreciate your
reviewing this matter once more and providing me with a
more suitable answer than the one I received from Mr. Lang.

Yours truly,

H. H. Link

H.H. Link
Personnel Relations

Encl.

**Acknowledging
Apologizing
Buying Time
Complaining
Congratulating
Conveying Bad News
Conveying Good News
Criticizing
Expecting
Expressing Goodwill
Informing
Predicting
Recalling
Refusing/Rejecting
Regretting
Requesting
Suggesting
Thanking
Urging**

1. a) Which of the strategies on the right are used in this letter?
    b) What expressions are used to signal the strategies?
2. What is the main purpose of this letter?
3. How does the tone accomplish that purpose?
4. Do you think the general tone is appropriate? Why or why not?

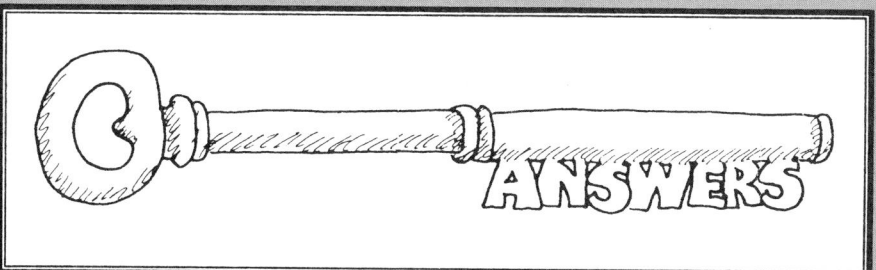

Memos 1.1 — **Page 6**

Jan.	Apr.	Sept. or Sep.	Nov.
Feb.	Aug.	Oct.	Dec.
Mar.			

Memos 1.2 — **Page 6**

Possible answers:

1987-02-14	1986-12-02	1987-09-05
1988-04-17	1985-01-26	1986-03-04
1988-08-25	1989-02-21	1989-02-14
1984-11-08		

Memos 1.3 — **Page 7**

1. Transfer Policy
2. On-the-Job Training for PM-01's
3. Human Rights Legislation
4. Delegation of Authority
5. Use of Taxis
6. End-of-Year Report
7. Energy Conservation Regulations
8. Unit Activities in March 1985
9. Copies for Canadian and Foreign Staffs
10. 1985-1986 Fiscal Year Close-off
11. Farewell Reception for Mr. J. B. Jones
12. Request for Lateral Transfer
13. Time-Related Efficiency Index
14. Cross-Analysis of Cultural Pastimes of Franco-Ontarians

Memos 1.4 — **Page 7**

Suggested answers:

1. Christmas Party Questionnaire
2. Guide and Form for Research Contractors
3. Heating System Maintenance (Place du Portage)
4. Language Training in Regina
5. Emergency Cheque Issuance

Memos 1.5 — **Page 8**

Suggested answers:

1. Vocational Guidelines Service
2. Security of Files
3. Notice of Meeting
4. Monthly Reports (July-December 1984)

Memos 1.6 — **Page 8**

Suggested answers:

1. Bicycle Storage
2. Temporary Assignment of J. Maloney
3. Postponement of Tuesday Meeting
4. Request for Annual Leave
5. Departure of Tara Farber

Memos 1.7 — **Page 9**

Possible answers:

1. Long	5. Short	8. Short
2. Short	6. Short	9. Long
3. Long	7. Long	10. Long
4. Long		

Memos 2.2 — **Page 13**

1. b or a   2. d   3. c   4. a or b

Memos 2.3 — **Page 13**

1. I hope this will be helpful to you. / I hope this will be useful to you.
2. I hope this will be helpful to you. / I hope this will be useful to you.
3. I hope this meets with your approval.

Memos 2.4 — **Page 14**

Possible answers:

1. With regard to your request of 1987-12-01, this confirms that Theatre Room 600 will be reserved for your group from 10:15 to 12:00 on 1987-12-09.
2. Further to our recent conversation about conflict of interest guidelines, this to confirm that . . .
3. With regard to your call about the January report, I would like to confirm that . . .
4. Following our telephone conversation of June 15, this is to confirm that summer hours . . .

Memos 2.5 — **Page 15**

1. b   2. d   3. a   4. c

Memos 2.9 — **Page 18**

Suggested answers:

1. will be studying / will inform you / as soon as possible
2. has been placed on the agenda / the next meeting / will be given careful consideration
3. have written / will forward their replies
4. will be considered / before / any final decisions
5. will let you know / as soon as
6. will be undertaken / as soon as / necessary

Memos 3.1 — **Page 20**

Possible answers:

1. This is to inform you that . . . / For your information . . .
2. Please note that . . .
3. Would you please note that . . . / Please note that
4. This is to inform you that . . .
5. For your information . . . / Please note that . . .

Memos 3.2 — **Page 20**

Possible answers:

This is to inform you that we have received the publication which you requested. You may pick it up at your convenience at the library any time between 8:30 and 4:30. We are pleased to have been of service.

Please note that the annual golf tournament will be held on June 28. All those interested in participating should phone Lynn Clarey at 993-1573. We look forward to a repetition of last year's great success.

Would you please note that there will be a fire drill today at 3:45. You are requested to leave the building as quickly as possible, using the staircase. Your co-operation would be appreciated.

Memos 3.4   Page 22

1. a (b,c)   2. d   3. b   4. e (c)   5. c

Memos 3.6   Page 23

1. I am writing to inform you . . .
2. This memo outlines . . .
3. My purpose in writing . . .
4. The aim of this memo is to . . . / The purpose of this memo is to . . . / This memo is to . . .

Memos 3.7   Page 23

Suggested answers:

1. The purpose of this memo is to inform you that the department's policy . . . / The purpose of this memo is to tell you that the department's policy . . .
2. The aim of this memo is to outline the main factors . . . / The aim of this memo is to describe the main factors . . . / The aim of this memo is to inform you of the main factors . . .
3. This memo outlines a number of directions which we might take in future and attempts to stimulate discussion of these directions.
4. This memo outlines the budget reporting schedules . . .

Memos 3.8   Page 24

Suggested answers:

1. d   2. a   3. c   4. e   5. b

Memos 3.9   Page 24

Possible answers:

1. c   3. b or c   5. a   7. a
2. b or c   4. c   6. c   8. c

Memos 3.10   Page 25

Possible answers:

1. b   3. b   5. a   7. b
2. a   4. b   6. b   8. b

Memos 3.12   Page 26

Possible answers:

1. Further to / your attention is directed to
2. In response to / I would like to point out that
3. In connection with / I would like to point out that
4. In response to / (No pointing-out expression)
5. With regard to / I would like to point out that

Memos 3.13   Page 27

Sentence 2 can be improved: "With reference to my budget proposal of February 3, 1985, Section D, page 14, I would like to point out that clerical staff guidelines . . ." / "With reference to my budget proposal of February 3, 1985, I would like to draw your attention to Section D, page 14, in which I show that clerical staff allotments . . ."

Sentence 4 is wrong. Remove "I would like to point out that".

Memos 3.14   Page 28

Suggested answers:

1. We anticipate that . . .
2. We are confident that . . .
3. . . . seems to indicate that . . .
4. It appears that . . .
5. We hope that . . .

Memos 4.1   Page 30

Suggested answers:

1. a) comprehensive   d) valuable
   b) highly useful   e) excellent
   c) confident

2. I wish you every success . . .

3. Bronson would probably feel that Stevens was so impressed with her work that she forwarded it without permission, knowing that she would not object.

4. Formal and polite.

Memos 4.3   Page 31

Possible answers:

1. a) It is unfortunate that these figures, which you have taken so long to compile, give an incomplete picture of last year's expenditures.

   b) While I realize that it has taken a considerable time to compile these figures, they do not give a sufficiently complete picture of last year's expenditures.

2. a) I regret that Mr. Johnson does not have the capacity to work under pressure, although his performance is otherwise satisfactory.

   b) While Mr. Johnson has always shown himself to be a satisfactory employee, we would like to point out that he works best when not under pressure.

3. a) We are very disappointed with your unit's processing of the personnel files. For this reason, we are sending Mr. Malt to assist in streamlining your procedures.

   b) We are aware that your unit is under great pressure and has difficulty processing personnel files; in order to streamline this process, we are asking Mr. Malt to assist your staff in any way he can.

4. a) I am sorry that you have not understood my instructions for moving the telex machines. Please contact Public Works as soon as possible to arrange the move.

   b) There seems to have been some misunderstanding in connection with my instructions for moving the telex machines. Would you kindly contact Public Works as soon as possible to arrange for the move.

Memos 4.5   Page 32

1. A nomination for a training program
2. Thank you / I regret very much / is necessary to / should Mr. Osborne still be interested / I would suggest
3. By providing a second chance
4. Suggesting
5. Yes (See pages 12 and 92.)

Memos 4.7   Page 34

1. extensive
2. a) please feel free
   b) Whatever you decide
3. a) much more than / exhaustive
   b) thorough / up-to-date / "devoutly to be wished"
4. that we limit ourselves . . . strictly
5. It softens the criticism by agreeing with a proposal previously made by Haynes.
6. Formal but enthusiastic

Memos 4.9   Page 37

1. we propose a new procedure / Future submissions should consist of / you should keep in mind that / It would, therefore, be prudent (The first three are extremely direct.)
2. The first sentence is direct but not annoying.
3. Formal and direct
4. The main suggestion is the list that gives details of what is to be submitted.
5. Steps to be implemented immediately

Memos 5.1   Page 40

THE SUBJECT

1. Yes
2. Yes, if paragraph 1 is changed (see LOGIC 1)

LOGIC

1. Paragraph 1 should not "congratulate" Smith but should "commend" her. The purpose of the memo is to deny the request.
2. Remove "Although"
3. The leave should be related to the work, not the work to the leave.
4. No. The memo refuses a request and needs no further comment.

GRAMMAR AND STYLE

1. "desire"
2. "a leave" should be "leave".
3. "not very much related" should be "not closely related".

TONE

1. The memo attempts to be polite and neutral.
2. Answers will vary.

Memos 5.2   Page 42

THE SUBJECT

1. Yes
2. Yes

LOGIC

1. To deny the request for education leave
2. "above" seems to refer to the Personnel Administration Act, but it may refer to the actual decision to deny the request.

GRAMMAR AND STYLE

1. "I regret to inform you that . . ."
2. Use "I" consistently, or modify paragraph 2 to make it clear that "we" is a committee.
3. "We feel" is inaccurate. The committee has judged the request according to clear guidelines. "We find that . . ."
4. ". . . and I would like to point out that you can apply for leave . . ."

TONE

1. Yes

A COMPARISON

2. The memo in Exercise 5.2 is better than the memo in Exercise 5.1.

Memos 5.3   Page 44

THE SUBJECT

1. No. The words "Comments on" are unnecessary.
2. The memo does not comment on the "punch-in" system; it criticizes it.

LOGIC

1. It is not clear just what "a tighter control" refers to. The writer should have added a phrase to make it clear that the reference is to greater control of hours worked.
2. It is not absolutely clear. If the writer wants productivity incentives, then she or he does not want tighter control of work hours.
3. Yes. It seems the suggestion is to create incentives for greater productivity and to hold a meeting to discuss various possibilities.

GRAMMAR AND STYLE

1. No
2. No
3. It is clear but unnecessarily wordy. The memo is from one supervisor who wants all supervisors to discuss the system.
4. were adopted (was adopted)

TONE

1. Personal and direct
2. No. It is too colloquial.
3. No. "Personally" is both colloquial and unnecessary.
4. It should be "I think". The writer has thought about the problem and arrived at a reasonable alternative.

Memos 5.4   **Page 46**

THE SUBJECT

1. Yes, but "Work Area Noise" would be better.
2. Yes. It is unclear which work area is referred to. Yes.

LOGIC

1. It is unclear whether the floor plan was intended to solve the same problem. It seems unreasonable to suggest an old proposal without attaching a copy.
2. It should be to point out a problem and to suggest a solution.

GRAMMAR AND STYLE

1. The double use of the pronoun is too direct and aggressive.
2. Answers will vary.
3. Since you hired
4. Omit "an".

TONE

1. Answers will vary.
2. Answers will vary.
3. Answers will vary. (Change "will" to "would".)

Memos 5.5   **Page 48**

THE SUBJECT

1. Yes
2. No
3. Yes

LOGIC

1. The memo does not state the date. It should be included.
2. "While" might be used.
3. The apology is inappropriate here. Omit it in this paragraph.

GRAMMAR AND STYLE

1. Should the budget be increased, I will gladly reconsider your request. / If the budget is increased, I will gladly reconsider your request.

TONE

1. Paternalistic
2. Try an expression of goodwill, or close with an apology.

Memos 5.6   **Page 50**

THE SUBJECT

1. Yes
2. Yes. However, it could include "late" or "overdue".

LOGIC

1. The paragraph does not make it clear that no payment can be made unless overtime schedules are received on the first Friday of the month.

GRAMMAR AND STYLE

1. I still have not received all your overtime schedules, although I requested them on March 4.
2. advance; otherwise, . . .

TONE

1. Both
2. Rude and abrupt
3. Answers will vary. (See RECALLING, page 24.)
4. Answers will vary.

Memos 5.7   **Page 52**

THE SUBJECT

1. No. The words "Comments on" are unnecessary.
2. No. It criticizes and offers two suggestions.

LOGIC

1. The main purpose was to have a boardroom and an interview room.
2. A boardroom and an interview room
3. The information should be stated clearly in the second paragraph.
4. It is not clear which floor is referred to. The writer should have indicated the floor number.
5. It is not clear which place is referred to. Reference should be to another floor or perhaps a different location.

GRAMMAR AND STYLE

1. Answers will vary.
2. "I think"
3. I can appreciate the difficulty of changing the floor plan . . .

TONE

1. It sounds too direct and therefore impolite.

Letters 1.1   Page 63

1. Comma after street number in French / period after abbreviation of Saint in English; hyphen in French / parentheses around province in French / hyphen in province in French
2. All words in titles capitalized in English; only first words and proper names in French / "Room", "Blvd.", and "W." capitalized; not "pièce", "boul.", and "ouest"

Letters 1.2   Page 64

1. Nfld./NF	6. Que. or P.Q./	10. Alta./AB	
2. Lab./LB	QC or PQ	11. B.C./BC	
3. P.E.I./PE	7. Ont./ON	12. N.W.T./NT	
4. N.S./NS	8. Man./MB	13. Y.T./YT	
5. N.B./NB	9. Sask./SK		

Letters 1.3   Page 64

1. Avenue	10. Court	18. South
2. Boulevard	11. The United	19. Northeast
3. Drive	States	20. Northwest
4. Street or Saint	12. Great Britain	21. Southeast
5. Place	13. Rural Route	22. Southwest
6. Square	14. Post Office	23. Suite
7. Crescent	15. East	24. Apartment
8. Road	16. West	25. Room
9. Parkway	17. North	26. Building

Letters 1.4   Page 64

Suggested answers:
1. Dr. / S.W. / Alta.
2. P.O. / R.R. / Cres. / B.C.
3. Ave. / N. / Ste. / Sask.
4. Ltd. / Blvd. / Alta.
5. P.O. / Blvd. / W. / Que. / Att:
6. Bldg. / Y.T.
7. P.O. / Ont.
8. Bldg. / Rm. / Rd. / N.S.
9. Bldg. / N.W.T.
10. Rm. / Bldg. / Rd. / Man.

Letters 1.5   Page 65

1. Letter	5. Letter	8. Letter
2. Letter	6. Memo	9. Letter
3. Memo	7. Memo	10. Memo
4. Memo		

Letters 1.6   Page 66

1. b	4. a	7. c	10. e	13. e
2. b	5. e	8. c	11. d	14. e
3. c	6. e	9. b	12. e	15. a

Letters 2.1   Page 68

1. c   2. b   3. e   4. a   5. d

Letters 2.2   Page 68

1. On October 18 we placed an order with your firm for a one-year subscription.
2. As I indicated during our discussions of May 9, I encourage the Bureau's participation in the following areas.
3. Please ensure that copies of all requisitions are sent to Mrs. Mackay.
4. This will acknowledge receipt of your letter requesting information on international travel by Ministers and Deputy Ministers since 1980.
5. Please be advised that, subject to Cabinet Document 1982-CCT-0641, the following policy changes will be implemented.

Letters 2.6   Page 70

has asked me to reply to / regarding / I am enclosing / I regret that / I hope that / Should you require / please do not hesitate

Letters 2.10   Page 72

Suggested answers:
1. I was delighted to hear that . . .
2. I would like to extend my sincere congratulations on . . .
3. It is my pleasant task to congratulate you on . . .
4. I would like to congratulate you on . . .

Letters 2.11   Page 73

Possible answers:
The first part of the letter is impersonal and could be interpreted as offensive; it would be more tactful to omit "basic". The second part attempts to be personal but does not succeed. The writer might have invited Mr. Williams to apply for future openings or suggested another department.

Letters 2.13   Page 74

Possible answers:
1. We regret that we are unable to fill your order until the beginning of the month.
2. Unfortunately we have to charge you for repairing the equipment, as the one-year guarantee has lapsed.
3. Since our deadline is January 26, we would very much appreciate a prompt reply.
4. I am sorry it has taken so long to reply to your letter, which reached this office only last week.
5. We regret to inform you that your request for education leave has been denied. If you wish to apply again, would you ensure that you submit a complete dossier.
6. The committee feels that there are a number of negative considerations that warrant the cancellation of this contract.

Letters 2.15 **Page 75**

1. Beginning   4. End   6. Beginning
2. Beginning   5. Beginning   7. End
3. End   or end

Letters 3.1 **Page 78**

1. b   2. c   3. a   4. d

Letters 3.2 **Page 78**

Possible answers:

1. I would like to draw your attention to the revised insulation standards . . .
2. You may be interested in knowing that the Deputy Minister has approved . . .
3. You may be interested in our recent publication . . .
4. I would like to draw your attention to the report of the regional transportation committee . . .

Letters 3.3 **Page 79**

Suggested answers:

1. It is recommended that / It is suggested that
2. We expect / We anticipate
3. I would advise
4. It would be advisable to
5. It is to be hoped that / It is anticipated that / It is expected that

Letters 3.5 **Page 80**

Suggested answers:

1. Acknowledging / Regretting, Informing / Suggesting / Thanking, Goodwill
2. The tone would be abrupt and impolite.
3. It is not essential, but it conveys goodwill.
4. She would probably have been offended.

Letters 3.7 **Page 81**

1. take steps / promptly
2. is anticipated
3. It is expected / will / important
4. There is an urgent need
5. I strongly urge
6. is urgently requested

Letters 3.8 **Page 82**

1. Your attention is directed to . . .
2. Direct and straightforward
3. I will expect / by August 1
4. Answers will vary.

Letters 3.9 **Page 83**

Suggested answers:

1. *Requesting:* We would appreciate
   Thanking: We are grateful for
2. Neutral and formal
3. Paragraph 2

Letters 3.10 **Page 84**

Suggested answers:

1. *Criticizing:* There seems to be a lack
   Urging: Your future assistance / would be greatly appreciated
2. Formal, direct, and abrupt
3. The briefness contributes to the abrupt tone.
4. Answers will vary.

Letters 3.11 **Page 85**

Suggested answers:

1. *Acknowledging:* This will acknowledge
   Buying Time: I regret that / are not available / at this time
   Informing: I am bringing / to the attention of . . .
   Predicting: I estimate that
   Apologizing: I apologize for
2. Yes

Letters 3.12 **Page 86**

Suggested answers:

1. *Recalling:* You will remember
   Requesting: I am writing to ask if you would
   Urging: we are in difficulty / we need
2. Urgent but polite
3. Answers will vary.

Letters 3.13 **Page 87**

Suggested answers:

1. *Acknowledging:* I have been asked to reply
   Informing: I am enclosing / the latter describes
   Suggesting: I would suggest that
2. Formal
3. Answers will vary.
4. Yes. I hope the enclosed information will be useful to you.

Letters 4.1 **Page 90**

Suggested answers:

Jack: I wish to thank you for your invitation.
Mr. Sawchuk: No closing is needed.

Letters 4.2 **Page 91**

Suggested answer:

If these arrangements are suitable, would you kindly let us know.

Letters 4.3 **Page 91**

Suggested answers:

1. a) In future, direct all questions of this type to . . .
   b) You might direct future questions of this type to . . .
   Please direct future questions of this type to . . .
2. You might get in touch with . . .
3. The staff there would be pleased to assist you.

Letters 4.4   Page 92

Suggested answer:

If you have any other questions, please get in touch with me again.

Letters 4.5   Page 92

Suggested answer:

I trust that these arrangements meet with your approval.

Letters 4.6   Page 93

1. I would appreciate receiving your comments on the proposed form before May 1.
2. Once again, I regret any inconvenience this delay has caused.
3. I will get in touch with them so that we can improve our understanding of the issues.
4. I would appreciate hearing from you by the end of April.
5. I would appreciate your attending to this matter at your earliest convenience.
6. If you need any further information, please do not hesitate to contact me. / Please do not hesitate to contact me if you need any further information.
7. If you have an alternate suggestion, we would be pleased to consider it.
8. We will send you the results of the competition as soon as possible.
9. I trust this information will be of some assistance to you.
10. I hope this explanation will answer the questions you raised.

Letters 4.7   Page 94

1. C	6. C	11. C	15. B
2. C	7. B	12. B	16. BC
3. B	8. C	13. BC	17. C
4. C	9. C	14. BC	18. BC
5. C	10. B		

Letters 5.1   Page 96

Suggested answer:

Your letter of February 15 addressed to Information Canada has been referred to this office.

The information you are seeking is the concern of several government departments, in particular the departments of Finance and of Energy, Mines and Resources, as well as the Privy Council Office. We are therefore sending a copy of your letter to each of these departments.

I am also enclosing a copy of *Our System of Government*, published by the Secretary of State, which may be of some assistance to you.

Letters 5.2   Page 97

Suggested answer:

This will acknowledge receipt of your recent letter requesting information on immunization procedures preparatory to your trip to Burkina Faso.

You are required to be in possession of a valid International Certificate of Vaccination against Yellow Fever. In addition, this department recommends that all travelers to this region be protected against polio, tetanus, and hepatitis A. The vaccination booklet is available from your doctor.

Please note that the record must include the name of the person vaccinated, the date of vaccination, the doctor's signature (with an indication of his or her professional status), and the origin and batch number of the vaccine used. Finally, the booklet must be submitted to a municipal, provincial, or federal health authority for application of the official validating stamp.

We trust this is the information you require.

Letters 5.3   Page 98

Suggested answer:

Thank you for your letter of October 31, 1987, regarding automobile parts manufacturers interested in exporting to Spain.

Unfortunately, I cannot give you an adequate answer without knowing what type of automobile parts your client is interested in. It would also be helpful to know whether your client requires parts for automobile assembly or for the service market.

When we have received this information, we will be in a better position to advise you of companies looking for export opportunities in Spain.

Letters 5.4   Page 99

Suggested answer:

Your recent letter to Indian and Northern Affairs Canada has been referred to this office.

I enclose our publications list and two booklets dealing generally with farming in Canada. I will gladly send you more specific information if you can provide details of your farming operation and of the problems you have encountered.

I look forward to hearing from you again.

> Sincerely yours,
> (Name)

Studying Memos & Letters 1   Page 114

Possible answers:

1. *Acknowledging:* In reply to
   Informing: I attach
   Requesting: Please see
   Informing: After completion . . .
2. Polite and neutral
3. The memo is sufficiently clear and polite that it does not need a closing sentence.

Studying Memos & Letters 2   Page 115

Possible answers:

1. *Acknowledging:* In answer to
   Informing: we have pleasure in / We have also contacted
   Expressing Goodwill: We hope this information will be useful to you.
2. Polite and neutral
3. Answers will vary.
4. Yes. We hope this is the information you require.

Studying Memos & Letters 3   Page 116

Possible answers:

1. *Acknowledging:* Further to our telephone conversation
   Informing: You will find attached
   Expecting: It is my understanding
2. Yes
3. The purpose of the whole sentence is to remind Conklin that he or she is expected and has agreed to send on the material.
4. No. The purpose of the memo is merely to accompany the enclosure.

Studying Memos & Letters 4   Page 117

Possible answers:

1. *Acknowledging:* This is in answer to
   Informing: states . . . / Enclosed is
2. The writer provides three sources of information and mentions two others. The memo contains a great deal of information. Its purpose is to inform.
3. Polite and informal
4. Yes. I hope this information will be helpful to you.
5. The informal tone is partly the result of vocabulary and grammar choices (a good deal of / If not, / and we will order) and partly due to the loose organization of the memo.

Studying Memos & Letters 5   Page 118

Possible answers:

1. *Acknowledging:* I refer to
   Informing: (No specific expression)
   Suggesting: It is quite possible
   Informing: it is a fact that
   Expressing Goodwill: Please advise . . .
2. It was damaged.
3. It was out of position and under water.
4. Cosgrove speculates that the marker may have been responsible for the damage. The purpose of the memo is to inform Preville of Cosgrove's evaluation of the facts available.
5. Polite and neutral

Studying Memos & Letters 6   Page 119

Possible answers:

1. *Acknowledging:* In a memorandum dated
   Informing: As far as the . . . is concerned, I think one could say that
   Refusing/Rejecting: but we are not staffed to
   Suggesting: We could, however, participate
2. The branch provides advice rather than hard information.
3. Formal and cautious
4. Formal: memorandum / on a consultative basis / to perform such a function / in any extensive way
   Cautious: I think one could say that / On occasion, I would imagine / could be made available

Studying Memos & Letters 7   Page 120

Possible answers:

1. *Acknowledging:* This refers to your memo of
   Informing: I am attaching copies of / Briefly / This has now / This developed / It is further pointed out that / Also enclosed
2. It was closed because of the danger caused by light aircraft landing on a beach used by campers.
3. No. The memo supplies factual information on the request of a superior.
4. A closing such as "I hope that . . ." might suggest that the field officer was not sure of the completeness of the information.

Studying Memos & Letters 8   Page 121

Possible answers:

1. *Informing:* I am enclosing
   Suggesting: except that provision should be made
   Informing: The document should be
   Requesting: We would appreciate
2. As Loken has been away, it might be wise to indicate which easement agreement is referred to.
3. The memo is neutral and polite, although it may contain an implied criticism.

Studying Memos & Letters 9   Page 122

Possible answers:

1. *Acknowledging:* Your January 27 memo
   Refusing/Rejecting: I should not wish to
   Informing: I enclose
   Buying Time: I have announced / it will contain
   Expressing Goodwill: I hope . . . is still open
2. The implication is that a clear answer is neither possible nor appropriate.
3. Direct
4. An expression of regret might make the refusal more polite.

Studying Memos & Letters 10   Page 123

Possible answers:

1. *Acknowledging:* I have recently received
Requesting: would it be possible / May I
suggest / I would also like to suggest
Urging: for this reason, an early reply would be
helpful
2. Yes. Bhattacharya says that the list is useful but
wants much more.
3. The memo is neither informal nor neutral. Bhattacharya disguises direct requests as suggestions so that the memo is polite, not aggressive.
4. Yes

Studying Memos & Letters 11   Page 124

Possible answers:

1. *Acknowledging:* I am writing in reference to
Informing: We have been informed
Requesting: We must therefore request
2. The tone is polite, neutral, and factual and seems
appropriate for a relatively straightforward issue.
3. The letter has enough detail.
4. A closing paragraph seems unnecessary.

Studying Memos & Letters 12   Page 125

Possible answers:

1. *Informing:* I am writing with regard to
Urging: overdue / I would urge / Furthermore, it
is essential
Expressing Goodwill: Thank you for your
cooperation in this matter.
2. The letter is abrupt.
3. Suggesting expressions would make the tone
less abrupt but would weaken the urgency.
4. A closing such as "I look forward to an early
reply" would maintain the logic and tone, but it
would make the letter even more abrupt.

Studying Memos & Letters 13   Page 126

Possible answers:

1. *Acknowledging:* Thank you for your letter
Informing: I have forwarded
Conveying Bad News ⎰ Unfortunately, at the
Refusing/Rejecting ⎱ present time I do not
anticipate / perhaps . . . will contact you if . . .
Expressing Goodwill: May I take this
opportunity . . .
2. Thanking someone for her or his interest is
usually a closing; here it is in the first sentence.
3. The intent is to make it clear that the refusal is
final, while maintaining a polite tone.

Studying Memos & Letters 14   Page 127

Possible answers:

1. *Acknowledging:* I am writing in reference to
Informing: Because of
Refusing/Rejecting: it would not be convenient
Suggesting: We would suggest
Requesting: would you kindly let us know

2. Formal and neutral
3. There is no statement of regret or apology. The
polite suggestion softens the effect of the
refusal.

Studying Memos & Letters 15   Page 128

Possible answers:

1. *Thanking:* Thank you for . . .
Expressing Goodwill: If my department can be of
any assistance
2. Thanking McLeod personally and on behalf of the
three representatives is appropriate. A third
expression of thanks would be excessive.
3. Personal

Studying Memos & Letters 16   Page 129

Possible answers:

1. *Acknowledging:* has asked me to reply to your
letter
Informing: A number of considerations / Thus, in
general
Suggesting: to refer you to
Expressing Goodwill: I hope this will be of some
assistance to you.
2. Yes. The tone is objective, dispassionate, and
formal, although there is a suggestion that Soper
is inadequately informed.
3. Yes. The use of "I hope" and of "some"
indicates that Larsen realizes that he or she has
not completely satisfied Soper's expectations.

Studying Memos & Letters 17   Page 130

Possible answers:

1. *Acknowledging:* This is in reply to
Informing ⎰ I must explain / somewhat at a loss to
Criticizing ⎱ understand
Informing   ⎰ This department is in no
Refusing/Rejecting ⎱ way / at no time was the
department authorized
Informing: I should also point out that
Refusing/Rejecting: In the circumstances, I fail to
see
No listed strategy: I can assure you (This is clearly
a warning.)
2. Angry and critical
3. It seems that Inlet Packing Ltd. has been taken
over by the Eastern Marine Trust Company. Rose
has written to the Special Services Division claim-
ing an amount that would have been paid to Inlet
Packing Ltd. He very likely used the words "sub-
sidy" and "obliged".
4. Yes. Lawrence believes that the trust company is
trying to defraud the government.

Studying Memos & Letters 18   **Page 131**

Possible answers:

1. *Acknowledging:* I have carefully reviewed

    Informing ⎱
    Rejecting ⎰ As for . . . I must inform you

    Informing (also promising): you may rest assured
2. The principal points in a grievance
3. The first sentence of the final paragraph could
    have expressed goodwill and good news.
    However, Fehr has chosen to use an indifferent
    tone throughout the paragraph.
4. Any conventional closing expression would be in-
    appropriate, given the indifferent tone of the letter.
    If it were to be rewritten to make the refusal more
    palatable for Collins, then a closing expression
    might help to make the tone more personal.

Studying Memos & Letters 19   **Page 132**

Possible answers:

1. *Expressing Goodwill:* I quite agree with you that
    Apologizing (and accepting responsibility): It is ob-
    vious that no excuse can be made
    Informing: First, there is the matter of
    Informing (and accepting responsibility): However,
    the fact remains
    Expressing Goodwill: I can only assure you that
    corrective action has been taken.
    Informing: The matter of
    Predicting: It is expected that
    Regretting: I regret that
    Apologizing: Once again, may I offer you my
    sincere apologies
2. The large amount of information is intended partly
    to persuade Brookes that he is not being given a
    bureaucratic brush-off and that something is really
    being done, partly to distribute the blame for what
    has occured, and partly to convince Brookes of
    Newton's and the department's goodwill.
3. The tone is persuasive and sincere.
4. Yes. Newton saves her strongest expression of
    apology until the end, where it seems to make
    the best impression.

Studying Memos & Letters 20   **Page 133**

Possible answers:

1. *Recalling:* Further to my letter to you on

    Criticizing ⎱ I am not satisfied with / It should
    Complaining ⎰ be clear

    Complaining: The continued delay / serve no
    useful purpose
    Urging: I would appreciate your
2. The main purpose is to urge Britnell to overrule
    Lang.
3. The tone is abrupt and critical. The letter is in-
    tended to provoke Britnell to act.
4. Answers will vary.

SELECTED REFERENCE BOOKS

Arnold, John, and Jeremy Harmer. *Advanced Writing Skills.* London: Longman, 1978
   A general writing coursebook integrating functions and grammar

Azar, Betty S. *Understanding and Using English Grammar.* Englewood Cliffs, N.J.: Prentice-Hall, 1981
   A structural grammar with many practice exercises

Bryson, Bill. *The Penguin Dictionary of Troublesome Words.* Harmondsworth, Middlesex: Penguin, 1984
   A usage guide with many examples from American and British newspapers

Capisto-Borde, Constance, and Sheila Malovany-Chevallier. *My English is French.* Paris: Albin-Michel, 1983
   A reference and exercise book on common French-English grammatical interference problems

Corder, J.W., and W.S. Avis. *Handbook of Current English.* Canadian Ed. Toronto: Gage, 1979
   A guide to standard Canadian writing style

Dart, Allan K. *ESL Grammar Quiz Book.* Englewood Cliffs, N.J.: Prentice-Hall, 1982
   A quiz and exercise book on English grammar

Department of the Secretary of State of Canada. *The Canadian Style.* Toronto: Dundurn Press, 1985
   The official Canadian government style guide

Gowers, Sir Ernest. *The Complete Plain Words.* Harmondsworth, Middlesex: Penguin, 1973
   A classic on civil service writing

Kirk-Greene, C.W.E. *French False Friends.* London: Routledge and Kegan Paul, 1981
   A contrastive dictionary of French-English cognates

Messenger, William E., and Jan de Bruyn. *The Canadian Writer's Handbook.* Scarborough, Ont.: Prentice-Hall, 1980
   A general guide to the grammar, mechanics, and usage of writing in English

Paxson, William C. *The Business Writing Handbook.* Toronto and New York: Bantam, 1981
   A reference for a wide range of business writing problems

Strunk, William, Jr., and E.B. White. *The Elements of Style.* 3rd Ed. New York: Macmillan, 1979
   A brief guide to usage and style

Thomson, A.J., and A.V. Martinet. *A Practical English Grammar.* 3rd. Ed. Oxford: Oxford University Press, 1980
   A structural grammar (exercises available separately)

Thomson, A.J., and A.V. Martinet, translated and adapted by G. Hardin. *Grammaire de l'anglais d'aujourd'hui.* Paris: Oxford University Press and Presses Pocket, 1984
   A translation/adaptation of the second edition of A Practical English Grammar

Webster's New Dictionary of Synonyms, Springfield, Mass.: Merriam, 1978
   A synonyms dictionary that explains differences of meaning